BECOMING FULLY HUMAN

BECOMING FULLY HUMAN

THE GREATEST GLORY OF GOD

JOAN CHITTISTER, OSB

A SHEED & WARD BOOK

ROWMAN & LITTLEFIELD PUBLISHERS, INC.
Lanham • Boulder • New York • Toronto • Oxford

A SHEED & WARD BOOK

ROWMAN & LITTLEFIELD PUBLISHERS, INC.

Published in the United States of America
by Rowman & Littlefield Publishers, Inc.
A wholly owned subsidiary of The Rowman & Littlefield Publishing Group, Inc.
4501 Forbes Boulevard, Suite 200, Lanham, Maryland 20706
www.rowmanlittlefield.com

PO Box 317
Oxford
OX2 9RU, UK

British Library Cataloguing in Publication Information Available

Library of Congress Cataloging-in-Publication Data Available
1-58051-146-5

Printed in the United States of America

♾™ The paper used in this publication meets the minimum requirements
of American National Standard for Information Sciences—Permanence of
Paper for Printed Library Materials, ANSI/NISO Z39.48-1992.

For Judy Allison,
whose beauty lies
in bringing the consciousness of beauty
to others,
whose insight brings
fresh vision
to my words.

CONTENTS

INTRODUCTION

When it comes to living through today, there are very few volumes to which a person can turn for help. When it comes to making choices between the good and the better in life, we don't get much information on how to choose between the two.

The situation strikes a strange note in the human heart. After all, life is about life. Why do so few even attempt to talk about the deep-down little things that make the difference between an active person and a spiritual person, between the life of the body and the life of the spirit?

The world is full of great theological tomes, of course. They talk about exalted things like life after death or the divine inspiration in Scripture or actual grace or original sin. They define God or dissect reason or struggle with the nature and state of revelation. They lead us to think about the end of life and the beginning of eternity. They lift us to the loftiest levels of human existence.

But at the end of the day, we are all still just where we were when we started: struggling with the mortgage, making career decisions, worrying about the state of our national affairs.

Then, those are the times when we feel least sure of ourselves. Are we ourselves really leading a good life? Here in the morass of every day, here where we feel overwhelmed and powerless and confused, with what do we measure our own lives?

I wrote this book to talk about times like those.

I mean this book to ask the simple questions of life, to etch out at least a beginning of the kinds of answers that make sense of today and show a path, however dim, toward tomorrow.

It's meant to prompt a reader to think through everything all over again that we've ever been told that life was about. It sets out to encourage a person to take a new set of bearings. It hopes to point out that we all need to live more by values than we do by rules. It calls the soul to begin to reshape the world here and now, on the only blade of grass over which any of us has any influence at all.

To find the fullness of the human in ourselves, we need to ask ourselves some basic questions and then to reflect on the answers as they are evolving in us. Where are we at this stage of life in answering these things for ourselves? Where were we before? At what point on the moral compass would we like to be?

The questions I ask are basic ones:

What is a simple life in a world and a society where having enough is never enough? What's the value of simplicity? In fact, is there any value in simplicity of life at all?

In a world that can destroy itself a hundred times over, what do we mean when we talk about a "just" war? Technology being what it is now, can there really ever be any such thing again? But if not, what do we do about evil in the world?

What is the blessing of age in a youth-centered culture? Is it all over at thirty? Is the rest of life worth anything at all? What happens when there is apparently nothing left to strive for in life?

Is holiness rigorous attention to religious ritual, or is it religious attention to the value of life?

Where does nature fit into the spiritual life? Is it of God, in God, or extraneous to the God-life completely? What does nature say to us as human beings?

What can Christians learn from the other great religions and Scriptures of the world? Does God speak in only one voice, to one people, about one thing? Or is every religion a call to the mind of the One God?

When is care for the self—or care for the other—excessive? What is balance in life really all about? Is it selfish to take care of the self? Is it holier to take care of the other? And how do we know which is which?

If God is just, why does justice never come? How do we square patient waiting with righteous anger?

What does it mean to be faithful? When should we simply admit defeat and move on?

What is enlightenment, and how does it happen?

How can we possibly be grateful to a giving God in the midst of violence, suffering, and loss?

When life is made up of nothing much but little things, do little things really matter?

The purpose of this little book is not to end thinking. It is to begin it. We live in a world consumed by things. Ideas too often get very short shrift. And so, then, do our souls, our heart, our humanity, and our life.

Read this book, then, not to learn but to develop your own ideas about the place of God, people, things, and the fullness of the human in your own life.

WHAT IS A SIMPLE LIFE?

Matthew 6:30

*If God so clothes the grass of the field, which is alive
today and tomorrow is thrown into the fire, will
God not much more clothe you?*

There is a story in the annals of monastic literature that has always both charmed and troubled me.

Once upon a time, this story tells, a seeker stopped at the cell of one of the monastics of the Egyptian desert seeking a word from the Spirit.

But when he entered the old monastic's cell, the seeker was shocked at the sight of it. In the cell were a mat, a table, some utensils, a book, and a prayer corner. Nothing else. Not one thing else.

"Where is your furniture?" the seeker said.

"Well, where is yours?" the monastic answered.

"Why would I have furniture?" the seeker said. "After all, I'm only passing through."

"Exactly," the old monastic said. "And so am I." Is that it? I asked myself. Is that simplicity of life? Is simplicity "poverty," and is poverty a virtue? And, if so, what good is poverty when people everywhere—including here in the richest country of the world—are dying because of it?

I've given a lot of thought to this topic—not simply in regard to you and your life but with my own life in mind as well.

After all, as I write to you about simplicity, my CD player is playing a Bach violin concerto softly and the fireplace glows behind me. And fireplace and quiet notwithstanding, I spend hours on the phone talking to technicians as I try to arm-wrestle into compliance the little three-pound computer on which I now write since I long ago put away my yellow pad and ballpoint pen.

What is simplicity of life? And is it possible at all anymore in a culture surrounded by the gadgets—the food processors and microwave ovens and cell phones and camcorders and e-mail and UPS tracking systems—that we never actually foresaw but now can't live without?

It all depends on what you mean by "simplicity of life." I myself am less sure than ever that what we have called simplicity in the past has ever really been simplicity at all. Deprivation, maybe. The cultural norm, maybe. But simplicity? Not necessarily. Not in the spiritual sense of the word. Not in the way the ancients used it, at least.

❧

Simplicity is a talent for going with the flow in life. When we have to affect our simplicity—plan it, impose it, strategize it—we're in real trouble. "There is more simplicity in the one who eats caviar on impulse," Chesterton wrote, "than in the one who eats Grape-Nuts on principle."

❧

If simplicity doesn't have more to do with living well than with the number of things we own, it is a virtue only for those who have things to forgo.

❧

G. C. Lichtenberg wrote, "The 'noble simplicity' in the works of nature only too often originates in the noble short-sightedness of those who observe it." Even the one-celled organism is made up of atoms and molecules beyond count. Simplicity doesn't really exist, in other words. We make it up. It's a sobering thought, spiritually as well as scientifically.

❧

Life is not simple. There is no controlling it, no shaping it in the style of a slower, calmer, idyllic world—long gone, if ever here. Instead, we need to learn how to deal with our complexities with simplicity.

❧

Life without necessities—grueling, unfair, and involuntary poverty—is not simplicity at all. Life without its essentials is, in fact, social obscenity, a moral responsibility that is incumbent on society at large. God judges the poor on their honesty but the comfortable on their generosity.

❧

Simplicity of life is more what poet Sister Madeleva Wolff, CSC, called "the habitually relaxed grasp" than it is life without gadgets that we never really wanted in the first place but realize are now part of the air we breathe.

❧

Simplicity of life is the ability to handle with single-minded unity of soul and serenity of heart whatever life brings.

❧

When our well-intentioned vegetarianism becomes rigid to the point that it puts other people under a great deal of strain cooking for us, how simple is that?

❧

When we handle our own life schedule very well because we refuse to have our own priorities interrupted by anyone else's needs, is that simplicity of life?

❧

Who is really living a simple life, the people with controlled menus, controlled physical environments, and controlled schedules or the people whose lives are twisted and stretched to make that kind of simplicity possible?

❧

Simplicity of life in a complex and complicated world is marked by four characteristics: It is honest, detached, conscious, and serene. Simplicity is an attitude of heart, not a checklist of belongings. Or, as Art Buchwald wrote, "The best things in life aren't things."

❧

Simplicity of life requires that we be honest about who and what we are. We live a simple life when we do not pretend to be something we are not.

❧

"In a consumer society there are inevitably two kinds of slaves," the social scientist Ivan Illich wrote, "the prisoners of addiction and the prisoners of envy." Simple people don't buy what they can't afford, or take on airs they haven't earned, or hide behind titles and pedigrees, masks, and patinas designed to protect us from the truth about ourselves.

❧

Everybody is "from" somewhere: from the broken family, from the alcoholic home, from the wrong side of town. It is those who reach back to where they're from to give a hand today to those who are also trying to grow beyond it, who live the virtues of simplicity of life.

❧

Simplicity has something to do with remembering who we are. It means being willing to have it known that I am from Bethlehem, not from Beverly Hills.

❧

Simplicity is authenticity. Etty Hillesum puts it this way: "Don't make ripples all around you; don't try so hard to be interesting; keep your distance; be honest; fight the desire to be thought fascinating by the outside world."

❧

Simplicity is not inverse classism, a kind of social pretense that is at base secure enough to risk nothing in giving something away.

❧

Simplicity is an attitude of mind that enables us to stand in the midst of our fine worlds sure of soul and unimpeded by the seductiveness of the unnecessary and the cosmetic.

❧

Simplicity is honesty, but it is also detachment. Honesty enables me to discover the hard truth that simplicity of life is not frugality of life: It is life unencumbered, life free of the things we own so that they do not own us. Jessie Sampter wrote, "Simplicity is the peak of civilization."

❧

"We own only what cannot be lost in a shipwreck," the Arab proverb teaches. That is hard truth in a consumer society whose economic base depends on the creation of false needs. We create what we do not need in order to keep our basic needs at bay.

❧

In a capitalistic society, if we don't buy, people don't work, and so the process never ends. So we "keep up" and we accumulate and we sink under the detritus of our own lives. Simplicity demands that we learn to live with open hands.

❧

Former Filipino first lady Imelda Marcos once responded to her critics by stating, "I did not have three thousand pairs of shoes. I had one thousand and sixty." We keep a dozen nonmatching water glasses for a house of three people "just in case." Simplicity is the ability to get rid of what we're not using rather than hoarding what we will never touch again.

❧

Whatever we now own is simply temporary. We're not taking it anywhere, so what is keeping us from being willing to get rid of it now? Perhaps the fear that real simplicity is an excursion into the trust that I will have what I need when I need it is too demanding of my soul to bear.

❧

Freedom is the real purpose, the real essence of simplicity. "Those who have cattle have care," the Kenyans say.

❧

Simplicity is openness to the beauty of the present, whatever its shape, whatever its lack. It enables us to be conscious of where we are and to stop mourning where we are not.

❧

Simplicity is not the arithmetic of the soul. Simplicity of life is not really about things at all. Simplicity is about being able to take them—and to leave them.

❧

Simplicity of life manifests itself in perfect serenity. The simple person pays close attention to the agitations that eat at the heart because it is our agitations that tell us where life has gone astray for us, become unbearably complex and eternally confused.

❧

Simplicity of life—purity of heart—centers us on the eternal that is in the now. The Bhagavad Gita says it like this: "To the illuminated man or woman, a clod of dirt, a stone, and gold are the same."

❧

There is no simplicity in a heart full of agitation and in a soul too distracted to recognize the one who is among us, yet invisible in chaos.

❧

Simplicity and serenity, simplicity and honesty, simplicity and openness, simplicity and acceptance are synonyms too long kept secret.

❧

Struck by a heart attack, a woman pleaded with God, "Oh, God, am I dying?" And God answered back, "No, no, no. You have thirty to forty good years yet. This is just a rehearsal." So, when she recovered from the heart attack, she decided to go for it. She stayed in the hospital, hired a plastic surgeon, had a face lift, a tummy tuck, a little breast augmentation and, the day before she left, brought in a cosmetologist to get her hair dyed. Then, she walked out of the hospital, was hit by an ambulance, and died. "God!" she squealed when she got to heaven, "I don't get it! You said I had at least another thirty years?!" And God said, "Yeah, that was the plan, all right. And believe me, lady, you would have got it. But when we got there, we didn't recognize you." As I was saying about simplicity, . . .

WHEN IS WAR UNJUST?

Isaiah 2:4

They shall beat their swords into plowshares, and their spears into pruning hooks;
nation shall not lift up sword against nation, nor shall they train for war again.

The Tao Te Ching, the ancient Chinese manual on the art of living, reads:

> Weapons are the tools of fear . . . a decent person will avoid them except in the direst necessity and, if compelled, will use them only with the utmost restraint. . . . Our enemies are not demons but human beings like ourselves. The decent person doesn't wish them personal harm. Nor do they rejoice in victory. How could we rejoice in victory and delight in the slaughter of people? Enter a battle gravely with sorrow and with great compassion as if attending a funeral. (ca. 550 B.C.E.)

Everywhere I go these days, people talk about being confused. Let me see if I can get it straight: The government is preparing the country for war with an "enemy" who has never attacked us. And we are going to allow this, presumably, because someone else whom we cannot identify, let alone capture, did attack us and the people we have decided to attack may attack us in the future. Right.

So, how does the average Christian think about something like this: as a citizen or as a Christian? And if as a citizen, does it reflect the best ideals of this country? And if as a Christian, on what criteria shall we base our conclusions?

The problem is not a new one. Over seven centuries ago, people began to recognize that war was an attack on the innocent by the ruthless for the sake of the privileged. They wanted it stopped. And if that was an unrealistic goal, given the thirst for power in the human condition and the absence of any overarching negotiating bodies, they at least wanted it regulated. They wanted the innocent protected. After all, the people were not fighting their neighbors. They wanted the defenseless made secure. After all, war meant that armies were to fight armies, not civilians. So they turned to the

13

church, which, by threat of eternal punishment, might be able to bring sense to chaos.

They popularized and developed the just war theory, first articulated by Augustine, and for a while it seemed to make sense. But over time everything has changed: the nature of the world, the nature of war, the nature of weapons, and the nature of nations themselves.

Adults seem to have a problem understanding such things. Children see it clearly: Some second-graders asked their teacher what was going on between the United States and the place called Iraq. So the teacher said, "Well, think of it this way: Somebody in your neighborhood has a gun in her house. All the neighbors are afraid of it, and they go to Margaret, the owner of the gun, to ask her if she'll get rid of it.

"And, Margaret said yes, she would. But after a while, the people began to doubt that Margaret had really thrown the gun away. So they went to see her again and asked her if she still had the gun. And she said yes, she did.

"So they told her that the fact that she had a gun made them afraid, so she had to get rid of it.

"But Margaret said no, she wouldn't because it was her house and her gun.

"So all the neighbors went back to their own houses, got out their own guns, pointed them at Margaret, and shouted that they would shoot if she didn't throw her gun away."

Then a child in the room spoke up and said, "Teacher, that is a really dumb story. It doesn't make any sense." Right.

When is war "just," or is war already obsolete now?

❦

"You can no more win a war than you can win an earth-quake," Jeannette Rankin wrote. But we go on trying. Why? What exactly is to be gained? The powerful stay in power. The innocent are expelled from their homes. Children grow up with fear and hatred in their hearts. Who wins what?

❦

For war to be just, the first criterion is that it must only be waged in the face of "real and certain danger." So when did we start waging war "just in case"?

❦

"All war is insane," Madeleine L'Engle wrote. Killing doesn't stop killing. It just gives the world a new reason to do it called "vengeance." In the meantime, the poor get poorer and the strong get stronger. Nothing really changes.

❦

After years of Nintendo and shopping mall video arcades, Americans know that no one bleeds and no one gets hurt in war. In fact, we teach our children to love it. Or, as Ellen Glasgow said, "The worst thing about war is that so many people enjoy it."

❦

War is not what happens in the military. It is what happens in the hearts of the rest of us who applaud it. Marianne Moore, the poet, wrote, "There never was a war that was / not inward; I must / fight till I have conquered in myself what / causes war, but I would not believe it."

❦

To be just, we're taught in the second criterion for a just war, war must be declared by "the competent authority." But

15

presidents no longer declare war at all. They simply ask Congress for the right to use "whatever force is necessary" to resolve an immediate problem. Or strike first and discuss it later. As Boake Carter put it, "In time of war, the first casualty is truth."

❧

Given the earth-shattering consequences of war in a high-technology society, no single government has the right to unleash a chain-reaction response without the consent and approval of the family of nations, all of whom will be affected by the disruption. War is not a backyard disturbance anymore.

❧

To be just, a war must pass the third criterion of the just war, the test of "comparative justice." The rights to be preserved must justify the killing that will be done in their name. So the question must be what rights do we as a people stand to lose if we don't go to war? And what rights have we lost that we must recover? Now there's a tough one.

❧

"All wars are popular for the first thirty days," Arthur Schlesinger Jr. wrote. Maybe that's why we unleash such murderous attacks against such unprepared opponents. Presidents know that on day 31 the clock begins to tick on popular support. Oil or no oil.

❧

For a war to be just, the tradition teaches, the fourth criterion is that "All peaceful alternatives must have been exhausted." Whatever happened to the days when cities weren't attacked, they were simply put under siege? Or has attack become too easy to bother engaging the soul and the mind in the task of preventing it?

❧

We need the kind of impatience, urgency, and outrage at the thought of war that our ancestors brought to the ideas of slavery, monarchies, and child brides. We need to begin to see the universal injustice of our current type of warfare, not to argue its justice.

❧

The fifth condition of the just war is "right intention." It can only be fought for a "just cause," a situation that outweighs the value of the number of lives that will be lost and the amount of damage that will be done in the waging of it. And what side that attacks first can ever plead "just cause"? To do that puts a nation in the place of God the Judge, a judge that punishes us before we even sin.

❧

"War is much too serious a matter to be entrusted to the military," a French proverb teaches. And that is surely true. But it may also be true that it ought not be trusted to legislators whose children will not be fighting it.

❧

"There is no such thing as an inevitable war," Andrew Law wrote. "If war comes it will be from failure of human wisdom." Maybe if we began to elect politicians for the quality of their imagination rather than on the basis of their experience we could find ourselves in a holier, healthier world.

❧

The sixth criterion of the just war is "the probability of success." No one is to rush a nation or a people into organized suicide, however noble the cause. But in this age, when nuclear and biological weapons stand at the ready, is any war anything but an invitation either to slaughter or to suicide?

17

❧

"Only two great groups of animals, men and ants," Charles H. Maskins wrote, "indulge in highly organized mass warfare." How do you like the company! And all this time they tell us how reasonable it is to hit them before they hit us. It makes you wonder, doesn't it?

❧

The final criteria of the just war are "proportionality and discrimination." The damage to be inflicted must be proportionate to the good to be achieved, and the innocent, the noncombatants, are to be spared. But we just finished bombing a country twenty-four hours a day for sixty days to catch one man—and missed him. The damage done, the innocent killed, the babies' eardrums that were shattered, the number of refugees created, and the body of villagers who starved from lack of supplies stand in mute testimony to the principle—or lack thereof.

❧

In an age when defoliation, ecological disaster, water pollution, starvation, and septic eruptions go on killing thousands for years after a cease-fire is finally achieved, how can any major military campaign be considered "proportional" anymore?

❧

The sad truth is that we prepare for war but not for peace. Or, to put it another way, what peace programs are being taught in our universities? What conflict-resolution courses are required in schools with ROTC programs? What scholarships are being given to those who major in programs in nonviolence? What's wrong with this picture?

❧

When did "militarism" become the only synonym for "patriotism"? And since when did plans to bomb cities full of babies and pregnant women become pro-life?

❧

"War is the science of destruction," John Abbott wrote. In a world where distance is no longer a defense against attack and bombing has become, in the words of United Nations observers, "apocalyptic," maybe it is time to stop giving war the benefit of the doubt. Maybe it is time to begin to think in terms of an unjust-war theory.

❧

Now that we fight our wars without body bags, from battleships hundreds of miles away from our targets or with clone airplanes and remote-controlled missile launchers, we have forgotten what war is really all about. We have become desensitized to the death of the other. Like Cain, we forget that we are meant, indeed, to be "our brother's keeper." But God is still counting their bodies.

❧

A "theory of the unjust war" would consider the long-term consequences of war on the innocent, the use of long-term commercial sanctions, the long-term effects of weaponry on an entire ecological region, an international review of grievances, international control of conflict resolution, and international sanction of the nations that supply weapons that make large-scale war possible in the first place.

❧

To destroy a country to punish a government is at the very least barbaric. Surely destruction of the quality of life for local noncombatants makes a war unjust.

❧

To rationalize the use of weaponry that is by its nature indiscriminate by calling the nonmilitary destruction "collateral damage" is doublespeak for slaughter. And the slaughter of innocents is unjust. Ask Herod.

❧

If armies want to fight armies, that may be one thing. If the old men who declare wars want to fight them face-to-face themselves, that may even be arguable. We can designate an empty field and they can go fight. When it's over, they can tell us who won.

❧

To send young men and women to destroy whole geographic areas with weapons no city can possibly defend against and call it "liberation" has got to be immoral.

❧

In a world where the long arm of international finance and commerce touches everyone and everything, war is both an unnecessary and inadequate method of dealing with national renegades. Boycotts brought South Africa to heel, and economic rejection led to the breakdown of the Soviet Union. War hurts the innocent; boycotts affect the people who stand to profit most from war—banks, businesses, and politicians. Maybe that's why we don't use them?

❧

Two final thoughts:

Will Rogers said once, "Diplomats are just as essential in starting a war as soldiers are in finishing it." Funny how that isn't funny anymore.

❧

If we want war to end, we will have to end it. For as Edmund Burke said, "No war can be long carried on against the will of the people."

WHAT ARE THE BLESSINGS OF DIMINISHMENT?

Psalm 23:6

Only goodness and kindness follow me
all the days of my life.

The average age of the population of the United States and most of Europe is thirty-five. The average age of the rest of the world is fifteen. And yet, in the United States at least, youth is the premium commodity. Age is a disease here. And aging is resisted at all costs. No other culture on earth disparages age the way we do. You have to wonder if we're not missing something.

The Hebrew Testament, for instance, sings to us, "To everything there is a season and a time for every purpose under heaven." Every stage of life, in other words, has its zenith, its gift, its joys, its struggles. But we don't talk about them much.

And the Zen master Huang-Po said, "Beginningless time and the present moment are the same. . . . You have only to understand that time has no real existence." But time is the Western obsession: We spend time, and save time, and lose time, and want time, and find time, and waste time, and give time, and take time. We are the only nation on earth that makes a person's age a necessary part of their identity. "Michael Sullivan, age thirty-eight," we read. "Melinda Wylie, age seventy-two," we say. And in the numbers, far too often, lies the value of the person.

The Buddha taught, "A self-sufficient person is a person who dwells in mindfulness. . . . He does not pursue the past nor lose himself in the future, because the past no longer is and the future has not yet come. Life can only take place in the present moment. If we lose the present moment, we lose life."

But when age is used as some kind of negative assessment, rather than as a gauge of gains, the present moment shrivels into insignificance. And we begin to hide its meaning in cosmetic surgery, and heavy makeup, and toupees, and bodybuilding exercises that become a way to deny who we are rather than simply to be as healthy as we can be.

But Jesus said, "I have come that you may have life, and have it more abundantly." Life is more than youth, it seems. It is abundant at all stages.

The Sufi tell the story of a king who gathered all the sages in the world to discover a ring that would make him happy when he was sad and calm when he was panicked. After months of prayer and charting of the stars and reading of tea leaves, the wise men came back to the king with a small, plain ring. "Your Majesty," they said, "here is the ring that will bring eternal peace to your life." At first the king was disbelieving, but then he came to understand. Inside the small gold band five words were engraved. They read, "This too shall pass away."

All of life is a series of gains and losses that comes with every stage of life. If we are living well, it is often difficult to tell one from the other. To gain one thing is to lose another. To lose something is to gain something else. The losses we weep over from generation to generation are often the greatest gains of our lives. It is the sign of the getting of wisdom to finally discover that.

ช

Getting old is life's last adventure. It is that time of life when we have everything we'll ever get. And that means that for the first time in life, we are free to enjoy every bit of it.

ช

Aging settles us. We walk more slowly, run more seldom, do less work. We are finally free to be who we are with the people we love.

ช

It isn't physical change that defines age. It's the realization that what we've built for ourselves is what we have. And what we've done to ourselves is what we have to enjoy.

ช

Age is the reminder that what we create inside ourselves when we're younger is what we will be left with in old age: a love for good music; hobbies that have captured our heart; friends who keep us alive in spirit; a passion for ideas and beauty and nature and life. Start now.

ช

The loss of one thing is always a call to develop something else. When our eyes begin to dim, we start to listen more. When our legs begin to go, we start to play chess. There is no such thing as losing life simply because we lose a piece of it. After all, there are many pieces of it that we're not using now as it is.

ช

The challenge of age is to keep a social life. "I used to think getting old was about vanity," Joyce Carol Oates wrote, "but actually it's about losing people you love. Getting wrinkles is trivial." Friendship is the treasure of age. Cultivate it.

❧

When we're young and running, we make acquaintances and ignore friends. Age is what teaches us to do otherwise, or we face the possibility of sitting alone in a room for years.

❧

Losing things is what enables us to begin again.

❧

Every stage of the human enterprise brings with it a task of its own. Concentrating on one stage and ignoring the next will only make the future more difficult to deal with because what we don't do today—establish personal control, develop emotional balance, learn how to deal with people, make career choices, contribute to the betterment of the world, get to know our children, take responsibility for our lives—will surely come to haunt every other period of life.

❧

Every stage of life has a joy of its own. Refusing to move on only denies us that new pleasure. "All sorts of spiritual gifts come through privation," Janet Stuart taught, "if they are accepted." But accepting them is the key.

❧

Every night before you go to sleep, ask yourself to name three good things that happened to you that day. Do it every single night, and getting up the next morning will be a gift, whatever its burdens. "If wrinkles must be written upon our brows," James Garfield said, "let them not be written upon the heart. The spirit should never grow old." Age is no excuse for being sour.

❧

The beautiful thing about getting older is that we want fewer and fewer of life's toys. It's what we have inside, not outside, that counts now.

❧

The Kenyans say, "Those who have cattle have care."
Once the stage of acquisition is finally over, we can get on
with the cultivation of soul in life. Then, we can forget about
becoming and start being.

❧

We adore youth, but few people would really want it
back again. It takes a while but eventually we learn, as Marie
von Ebner-Eschenback said, that "being young is beautiful,
but being old is comfortable."

❧

Age gives us the opportunity to consider what we learned
when we were younger. We can't use it now, of course, but it's
nice to appreciate it anyway. It makes us realize that it's all
been worth it.

❧

There is no such thing as loss. There is only the opportunity to begin again.

❧

It isn't that our losses do not bring us pain. It's that the
pain simply makes us remember what a blessing it was to
have had them.

❧

To be able to lose a thing without ever feeling the pain of
its going means it never meant anything to us to begin with.
And that is the mark of a totally empty life.

❧

Wisdom is when we know that everything we've ever had
or done has made us a better person, no matter how we resisted the doing of it then. Or, as Jean Paul put it, "The more

sand that has escaped from the hourglass of our life, the clearer we should see through it."

❧

Those who live in regret all their lives have ceased to live at all.

❧

It's not a matter of what we've done in life that counts. It's what we've learned from it that makes the difference between wisdom and experience.

❧

Never think that either getting or losing is in vain. Each of them teaches us a lesson. Getting teaches us that we didn't need it and losing teaches us that we grew from it.

❧

Middle age is when we know all the answers but no one asks us the questions anymore.

❧

Life is not a matter of winning and keeping. It is a matter of learning to go on. "Life only demands from us the strength we possess," Dag Hammarskjold wrote. "Only one feat is possible—not to have run away."

❧

Physical diminishment comes with a glow if our growing has been fruitful in every stage. "How beautifully leaves grow old," John Burroughs wrote. "How full of light and color are their last days."

❧

Life is a cycle of waxing and waning. The only problem is that we so often confuse one for the other.

ॐ

We set out to get one thing in life and wind up with the one we were supposed to have.

ॐ

Hysteria is a function of youth. Serenity is a mark of age. By that time we know that "this too shall pass."

ॐ

The function of age is to save us from our youth. Or, as Rabbi Nahman of Bratslav put it, "If you won't be better tomorrow than you were today, then what do you need tomorrow for?"

ॐ

Every mountain of every stage of life is to be conquered with a smile. That's what makes a person sweet. "We arrive as a novice," Sebastian Chamfort wrote, "at each stage of life." Everything has something to teach us. The only question is, Do we allow it, or do we resist it with all our might? In which case, we will manage to make every stage miserable.

ॐ

All of life, every minute and stage of it, is to be savored. As the poet Edna St. Vincent Millay said:

> I drank at every vine,
> The last was like the first.
> I came upon no wine
> So wonderful as thirst.

Live. Live. Live.

What Is Sanctity?

Matthew 5:48

*There must be no limit to your goodness, as our
God's goodness knows no bounds.*

Second grade is a very dangerous time in life. At least it was for me. I questioned everything. Sister taught us all about martyrs, for instance, and then asked how many of us would like to be one. Almost every kid in class put up his or her hand. Not me. I didn't think martyrdom was a good idea then, and I don't think it's a good idea now. "There has got to be an easier way to get to heaven than that," I thought. And there is.

Sister read to us from the Gospel of John. "Love God and do what you will," John said. That, I figured, I could do.

But then I got old enough, experienced enough, wise enough in the ways of the mystics to know what John really meant. It's not what we do that makes us holy. It's what we love that makes the difference between being simply a spiritual virtuoso and being a saint.

The Sufi understood the paradox very well. El-Ghazali, the great Muslim imam, told a story one day about Isa ibn Maryam: Jesus, Son of Mary. One day Isa saw a group of people sitting miserably on a wall, moaning out loud and full of fear. "What is your affliction?" he asked. "It is our fear of hell," the people complained.

Then Isa came upon a second group. They were emaciated and wan and full of anxiety. "What is your affliction?" Isa asked them. "Desire for Paradise has made us like this," the people cried.

Finally, Isa came upon a third group. They were scarred and bruised, wounded and tired, but their faces were radiant with joy. "What has made you like this?" Isa asked. And the people answered, "We have seen the Spirit of Truth. We have seen Reality," they sighed. "And this has made us oblivious of lesser goals."

And Isa said, "These are the ones who attain. On the Last Day, they will be in the Presence of God."

If we live our spiritual lives only in fear of punishment or in hope of reward, rather than in the awareness of the One because of whom all life is worthwhile, we can be religious people, but we will never be holy people. Then life is simply a series of tests and trials and scores, not the moment-by-moment revelation of God who is present in everything that happens to us, in everything we do.

Sanctity is about how we view life. It is not about spiritual exercises designed to evaluate our spiritual athleticism or a kind of spiritual bribery designed to win us spiritual prizes we do not deserve.

❧

Sanctity and sin are not incompatible. It's only when we refuse to learn from sin, when we become the sin rather than grow beyond it, that sin is a barrier to sanctity. Or, as Eric Hoffer put it, "Many of the insights of the saints stem from their experience as a sinner."

❧

I used to think that sanctity meant keeping the rules. Now I know that it means knowing the self. When I really know myself, I know what I must do to be the best me I can become. Then, it becomes impossible for me to judge another.

❧

The one who is holy sees God in everything in life and calls it blessing—even when it does not feel like blessing.

❧

Holiness lies more in forgiving the other than in not sinning oneself.

❧

To be holy, we must always do more than what is expected, and expect more than what is acceptable. Holiness goes beyond the adequate to the heroic.

❧

Holiness is not getting good marks on a heavenly report card. It is becoming as godlike—as kind, as just, as merciful, as loving—as we can be on earth. "There must be no limit to your goodness, as our God's goodness knows no bounds," Jesus teaches in the Sermon on the Mount. In other words, get real. Playing a game called religion is not what real holiness is about.

＊

We become holy when we recognize the Spirit of Truth in life—and live by it. The problem is that if this happens to you, you find yourself having to confront all the Hitlers of the world, as Dietrich Bonhoffer did. You find yourself having to resist all the oppressors of the world, as Martin Luther King Jr. did. You find yourself having to do something to care for all the poor of the world, as Dorothy Day did. You sometimes even find yourself in conflict with officials of the church, as Hildegard of Bingen did. Then holiness lies in choosing "reality" over being "realistic" enough to know that nothing can be done about those things. Or, as Hildegard herself said, "Holy persons draw to themselves all that is earthly."

＊

"Saints are nonconformists," Eleanor Rice Taylor wrote. That means, I think, that when the world is full of violence and greed and sexism and racism and you and I think just what everyone else thinks about those things, we have to ask ourselves when we chose the ways of the world over the mind of God. That's the moment we chose against holiness.

＊

God is present in everything around us, in everything we do, wherever we are, and in whatever situations we find ourselves. It is coming to a sense of the Presence of God that changes our attitude toward life. "Every day is a god, each day is a god, and holiness holds forth in time," Annie Dillard wrote.

＊

God uses time to shape us into living witnesses of eternal truth.

❧

Coming to know the sacred—the energy of air, the possibility in children, the beauty of regret, the value of life—is what makes us holy.

❧

Life lived without a sense of the holy-making mysteries of life is not life. It is an existence lived only at the level of the apparent. It starves the spirit and feeds it on the senses alone. It kills the soul and blinds the heart to everything that makes life worth more than the impermanence of the present moment.

❧

The holy person does not give donations to the poor; she becomes the voice of the poor. The holy person does not make just deals; he makes fair deals. The holy person does not give a just wage; he gives a living wage. Or, as the rabbis teach, "The righteous always give a little more than the scales indicate."

❧

Beware of the desire to be thought holy. "None attains to the Degree of Truth until a thousand honest people have testified that he is a heretic," the Sufi say. It's when we do what the gospel demands rather than what the law demands that we begin to feel the sting of sanctity.

❧

All of life is a struggle to become more than we are. We don't fail in that attempt often; we fail all the time. But that's not the point. The point is simply whether we accept the failure or not. No one is put out of Alcoholics Anonymous for failing to stay sober the first time he promised he would. "Virtue does not consist so much in abstaining from vice," W. T. Eldridge wrote, "as in not having an affection for it."

❧

Public propriety is the poorest of measures of sanctity. It's not what we look like in church that counts. It's what we are in our hearts that matters.

❧

"There is no sinner like a young saint," Aphra Behn wrote. We all grow up. Sin is not a terminal disease; it is a learning experience.

❧

To be holy is not to be without temptation. It is to be without love for the sin.

❧

Holiness requires that we face all our temptations. They tell us something about ourselves that we need to develop. Without those temptations we are only templates of what it means to be a real person.

❧

"How easy it is to be virtuous," Dolf Wyllarde said, "when we have no inclination to be otherwise." Just because you've never wanted to murder someone doesn't mean that you're a saint. It may simply mean that you're without passion for virtue. And that might be your real sin.

❧

The purpose of life is to let God work through us to make the world a better place for every living creature. Anything less than that which calls itself sanctity is only sham.

❧

If you don't see a lot of holiness and virtue around you, be careful not to tell anyone. As Henry David Thoreau said,

"That virtue we appreciate is as much ours as another's. We see so much only as we ourselves possess."

❧

It is easy to be virtuous at the expense of others. Children seem to know that intuitively. That's why they won't tell on one another. But adults are prone to outgrow that concern along the line. Then they turn their friends over to the power of the state or their neighbors in to the Inquisition. That's when virtue becomes what the philosopher Camus called "a principle of evil." Beware of it. It is the most insidious kind.

❧

When vice parades as virtue, there is no greater vice. When we make war on the defenseless in the name of defense and call it a good thing, we have confused justice and vengeance. When we use religion to be irreligious, God weeps.

❧

Those are holy who know that they have been brought into this world in order to do something for the rest of it.

❧

The publication of other people's vices is not a virtue. "Men's evil manners live in brass, their virtues / We write in water," Shakespeare noted. And that may be the most damaging vice of them all.

❧

The saint goes deeper and deeper into the mind of God and comes up thinking the same.

❧

It's so easy to be just like the crowd and so difficult to be just like the gospel. Or, as Mark Twain pointed out, "Be virtuous and you will be eccentric." On the other hand, be eccentric and you may find yourself up to your neck in virtue.

Religious rigidity is not virtue. It simply, as Jung said, "radiates an atmosphere of the torture which [the virtuous] inflict on themselves. This is not a virtue but a vice." Holiness is simply commitment to the Spirit of Truth when it would be safer to buy into the current social lie.

"Johnny, was it you who tipped over the outhouse this morning?" his father asked. And Johnny said, "I cannot tell a lie, Father. Yes, I tipped over the outhouse." "That's exactly what I thought," the father said, turning little Johnny over his knee. "But why are you spanking me?" Johnny cried. "I told the truth just like George Washington did when he told his father that he had cut down the cherry tree." "Yes, you did," the father said, rubbing his hands together. "But George Washington's father wasn't sitting in the tree when he did it!" As G. C. Lichtenberg said, "Virtue by premeditation isn't worth much."

How Is Caring for the Earth Spiritual?

Revelation 7:3

Hurt not the earth, neither the sea, nor the trees.

From where I sit on this Sunday morning, I can see the fish farm holding tank floating in the middle of the bay below. Every morning since I have been in Ireland, a small boat labors through the channel to service a set of them that shelter in the lee of the offshore islands. But not without concern. Attitudes here differ about the value of the process. Some of the villagers see the fish farms as a blight on the landscape, a pollution of the very waters fishermen say they are saving, thickening the ocean bed with the detritus of fish breeding, fish blight. Others here say it's the only way to make fishing a stable and profitable industry in an area where industry is lean.

At the same time, everyone agrees that problems of industrial poisons now threaten all the water on the planet and something must be done to preserve both fish and fishing. All of the people wonder which way is the best way to resolve it. The truth is that I don't know the answer to any of those questions. But one thing I do know: All of these people are asking questions because they love the land, they value the water, they respect the fish life, and they know themselves to be the species most dangerous and most endangered if the answer they arrive at is wrong.

They know, unlike so many city people, that what happens to the land and the water and the air happens to them. But however the questions are posed, the fact remains that they are not scientific questions at all. How to relate to the natural world around us is, in fact, the most ancient of spiritual issues.

The Buddhists tell it this way: Ryokan, a Zen master, lived the simplest kind of life in a little hut at the foot of the mountain. One evening a thief visited the hut only to discover that there was nothing there to steal.

Ryokan returned and discovered him in the act. "You have come a long way to visit me," he told the prowler, "and you should not return empty-handed. Please take my clothes as a gift."

The thief was bewildered. He took the clothes and slunk away.

"Poor fellow," Ryokan mused. "I wish I could give him the beautiful moon."

Ryokan gave the thief everything he had. What he could not give him—a stark and elemental grasp of nature, an appreciation of the beauty that is life—was what the thief needed most. It is what we may need most as well.

And Jesus said, "Look at the birds of the air; they do not sow or reap or store away in barns, and yet your God in heaven feeds them. Are you not of more value than they?"

· It's what we have when we have nothing that defines our relation to nature and the effect of nature on the soul. Then we begin to realize that we do not exist outside of nature or above nature or independent of nature; we are simply its most vulnerable part. What we learn from nature may make the whole difference in the way we go through life, and what we want from it, and what we consider important in it, and—most of all—what we are capable of learning by being alive.

Nature is what calls us to the center of our souls where the pristine, the primitive in us touches the pristine and the primitive in life. Where there are no words, there is only the option of understanding.

When you're in a forest, no amount of sophistication or rationalization can protect you from an awareness of what you really are—only a small part of life.

We are not pure spirit, sharp mind, angelic creatures. We are a soul wrapped round by a body that, like everything else, will someday go back to the earth with which, however much we would like to deny it, we are one.

Nature reminds us that there is no such thing as a static world. We are a bubbling, fomenting universe of bubbling, fomenting beings—the most changeable of which is ourselves. As Herbert Hoover said, "The natural world is dynamic. From the expanding universe to the hair on a baby's head, nothing is the same from now to the next moment." So why do we ever think that we can pin life down to our demands?

We are not simply physical organisms. We are the energy of the universe, focused in consciousness and encapsulated in a human body. It is into that energy that we shall someday melt and return.

The natural world shows us the vastness of the ecosystem, the glory of God, the possibilities of creation, the wonder of the universe. And here we are in the midst of it. How can we possibly say that life is bad?

❧

Anzia Yezierska wrote, "The power that makes grass grow, fruit ripen, and guides the bird in flight is in us all." The spiritual implications are clear: Life moves, and we must move with it.

❧

When we come into rhythm with the rest of nature, we come into contact with the deepest part of the self. The poet Lucille Clifton wrote, "I keep hearing / tree talk / water words, and I keep knowing what they mean."

❧

Nature is a Sunday school of spiritual lessons: grass teaches us that however frail the pieces of our life may seem, they persist in us; water that the basics of life sustain us, not its frills; mountains that every effort in life leads to another valley. The problem is that, too often, we fail to wonder what the life around us has to say to our own.

❧

The sheer perdurance of nature is what teaches us to go on. "Those who contemplate the beauty of the earth," Rachel Carson wrote, "find reserves of strength that will endure as long as life lasts." To immerse ourselves in pools of beauty enables us to bring beauty to the homeliest parts of our life.

❧

To watch a mountain stream wind its way around the boulders on the hill and the roots of hard trees and the bog of the meadow till at last it reaches the sea is enough to teach any of us to patiently, patiently work our way through the hard parts of life.

We are inclined to think, perhaps, that we are less rooted in nature than a tree simply because we can walk. But too often, unlike the tree, we fail to draw from our surroundings the very nourishment we need to survive.

Environmentalism is not an option. It is an exercise in self-understanding.

Nature restores the soul to its state of oneness with the universe. Nancy Wood wrote, "My help is in the mountains / Where I take myself to heal / The earthly wounds / That people give to me." The problem may be that the urban world does this far too seldom now.

Beware the ability to reason. It enables us to be the only part of nature that behaves unnaturally.

To appreciate nature is not the same as to pillage and plunder it. We have made war on nature and wonder why there is so little peace in ourselves when what we destroy is exactly what we need most.

Nature is God's way of teasing us to think beyond it. Or as Emily Dickinson wrote, "I hope you love birds, too. It is economical. It saves going to Heaven."

When we surround ourselves with nature, we become better people. "Arranging a bowl of flowers in the morning can give a sense of quiet in a crowded day—like writing a poem or saying a prayer," Anne Morrow Lindbergh said. We cannot expect to get lifted up out of the cesspools of life if we ourselves do not do the lifting.

It isn't that we are too natural that is our problem. Our problem is that we are unnaturally natural. We do to nature what nature would never do, and we do it in the name of being "reasonable." And so nature dies—and we die, too. Both spiritually and, now, physically, too.

In our need to distance ourselves from nature, we have become intellectual robots in a sea of cement. Who can think like a rose under those conditions?

Do not be surprised if people act like "animals" in a society too far removed from animals to understand their gentleness. Barbara Deming wrote, "We are earth of this earth, and we are bone of its bone. / This is a prayer I sing, for we have forgotten this and so / The earth is perishing."

When we learn to live in harmony with nature and not at war with it, we become more human in the process.

We were not created to fight nature. We were made to live in concert with it. But now we can't wait for lobster season to take our fill. We have to overproduce, overfish, and overstock a species until we manage to destroy it completely.

❧

Cows know that it's a good idea to stand with their backs to the wind. We insist on figuring out how to redirect the wind. "I like trees," Willa Cather said, "because they seem more resigned to the way they have to live than other things do." Who, us?

❧

When we deprive ourselves of the presence, the lessons, the beauty of nature we lose touch with the Spirit of Life. "If I had but two loaves of bread," the Koran says, "I would sell one and buy hyacinths for they would feed my soul."

❧

To be immersed in nature is to be immersed in the imagination of God. "All are but parts of one stupendous whole," Alexander Pope wrote, "whose body Nature is, and God the soul."

❧

To lack the natural in the spiritual life is to lack identity with the universe. But then how can we ever really come to know God? William Harvey put it squarely: "Nature is a volume of which God is the author."

❧

When we talk about "doing what comes naturally," we are usually talking about doing what makes a mockery of being human. "Accuse not Nature," Milton wrote, "she hath done her part; do thou but thine!"

❧

Woody Allen said of his allergies, "I am at two with nature." And therein starts the war between the human and the beast. But in the end, at the rate we're going with global warming and deforestation and desertification, the beasts will win yet.

❧

The tourist found the Indian chief lying flat out in the middle of the highway, ear pasted to the ground. The chief said, "Eight-cylinder, Plymouth, 1999." "You can tell the cars that are coming just by putting your ear to the road?" the tourist gasped. "No, you idiot," the chief said. "That's the description of the car that hit me!" When we label some people "natural," but not ourselves, we stand to miss a lot of information in life.

❧

The human species is the only part of nature that has a complete monopoly on the seven deadly sins—pride, anger, lust, greed, sloth, gluttony, and envy. Some distinction.

What Can Christians Learn from the Koran, Dhammapada, Bhagavad Gita, and Lotus Sermons?

John 17:21

That they may all be one, as you are in me and I am in you.

Scene 1: I was raised in the Roman Catholic world of the 1950s. Denominational lines were tightly drawn then. Theological insulation was the norm. Bigoted truisms abounded: Catholics learned that Protestants didn't go to heaven. Protestants learned that Catholics worshiped Mary. Both of them learned that the Jews killed Jesus. The Jews learned that Christianity threatened their very existence. And they all learned that everybody else in the world was "pagan."

It was all very neat. It was also very unholy. It served to compartmentalize both the world and God. It made God a tribal God. Truth was not one; truth was Catholic. Period.

Fast-forward. Scene 2: Vatican Council II publishes a document on ecumenism. Ecumenical dialogue—theological discussions in the whole Christian community, Catholic and Protestant—begins. And interfaith work—meetings of representatives of both Christian and non-Christian traditions—becomes a regular part of the religious landscape as well. Vatican II states in the document *Nostra Aetate*, "We must believe everything that is true in other religions." What? If we are to believe "all that is true" in other religions, something must be true.

Fast-forward again. Scene 3: It is 1995 and I become a founding member of the International Committee for the Peace Council, a body of high-profile religious figures from every major spiritual tradition in the world: Hindu, Buddhist, Jewish, Muslim, and Christian. For a professed representative of the Catholic ghetto, it is a shocking collection of Asian monks, Hindu swamis, Muslim imams, Catholic monastics, a Nobel Peace Prize–winning bishop, Protestant pastors, and religious scholars from every tradition. What can possibly be accomplished here?

One of the peace councilors is Maha Ghosananda. A small round man with round eyes and round head and round body, a veritable circle of orange sunburst, he smiles a glowing smile across the table. But he never says a thing. He just sits there in his orange robes cross-legged on the chair, looking seraphic, serene, very comfortable, and very out of place at the same time. He is some kind of living icon of peace, I'm sure, but just what I don't know.

All day he smiles and smiles as we discuss going, as a sign of religious unity, to places where religion is at the root of conflict: to Chiapas, to Belfast, to Jerusalem, to India. I begin to wonder what he possibly knows about all of this, if anything. When he's out of the room, we're told that he is the supreme Buddhist patriarch of Cambodia. This is the monk who has begun the dharma walks across the country to call attention to the minefields there that have crippled so many and killed even more.

Then, out of nowhere it happens. The reason he does it, they say, is because his family—his entire family: brothers and sisters, nieces and nephews, in-laws and distant cousins—was murdered in the Pol Pot regime. He has no one left in the world. No one at all. So he does it, because as a Buddhist, he must teach peace.

What can we learn from the spiritual heritage of other traditions? Answer: That God is in the heart of humankind, and if we listen clearly, we can hear that same voice in another language. These reflections deal with what Christians can learn from the Koran, the Dhammapada, the Bhagavad Gita, the Talmud, and the Lotus Sermons. Listen.

❧

Religion is meant to lead us to the center and source of creation. The aberration of religion, then, lies in spending so much time as religious people claiming our truth and condemning everybody else's.

❧

As Napoleon put it, "Theology in religion is what poisons are in food." When theology is used to condemn another person's path to God, it not only distracts us from the purpose of religion but distorts it as well.

❧

"It is better to light one small candle than to curse the darkness," Confucius said—not the Christophers. Now here's the really religious question: If the Christophers had identified the source of the quotation, would you, as a Christian, have accepted it? In fact, would you have accepted the Christophers?

❧

"Never in this world can hatred be stilled by hatred; it will be stilled only by nonhatred—this is the law Eternal," the Buddha said. "Love your enemies," Jesus said.

❧

"The breath of the flute player, does it belong to the flute?" the Sufi poet Rumi wrote. "And God breathed life into the clay," the Book of Genesis says. "In him we live and move and have our being," the Book of Acts tells us.

"God is the East and the West and wherever you turn, there is God's face," the Koran teaches. "Behold I am with you all days," the evangelist Matthew says, "even to the end of time."

❧

The Japanese teach that "forgiving the unrepentant is like drawing pictures on water." Jesus taught, "If you are offering your gift at the altar and there remember that your brother or sister has anything against you, leave your gift at the altar and go reconcile with them."

❧

The Hindu Upanishads talk about creation this way: "As its web a spider emits and draws in, just as plants arise on the earth and wither, just as hair develops on living persons, even so this world from the Self arises." The Book of Genesis says that God created all things.

❧

The Hindus teach, "May peace and peace and peace be everywhere." Jesus said, "Peace I leave with you, my peace I give to you." The overall message is clear: The abiding presence of God is a universal revelation.

❧

The Buddha said there is an Eightfold Path to inner peace: right view, right aim, right speech, right action, right living, right effort, right mindfulness, right contemplation. Jesus says there are eight beatitudes: mercy, poverty of spirit, mourning, meekness, hunger for righteousness, purity of heart, peacemaking, and witness. Do you think they decided on these together?

❧

"It is easy to see the faults of others," the Buddha said, "but difficult to see one's own faults. One shows the faults of others like chaff winnowed in the wind, but one conceals one's own faults as a cunning gambler conceals his dice." Jesus said, "Why do you see the speck in your neighbor's eye but do not notice the plank in your own?"

The Buddha taught, "Happy is he who has overcome his ego; happy is he who has attained peace; happy is he who has found the Truth." Jesus taught, "Unless you become as little children, you cannot enter the kingdom of heaven."

The Hindu Bhagavad Gita teaches, "These bodies are perishable; but the dwellers in these bodies are eternal, indestructible, and impenetrable." Jesus said, "This day you shall be with me in paradise."

"In this world aspirants may find enlightenment by two different paths," we learn in the Bhagavad Gita. "For the contemplative is the path of knowledge; for the active is the path of selfless action." The Christian tradition teaches that both contemplation and a commitment to social justice are essential parts of the Christian life.

"Forsaking egoism, power, pride, lust, anger and possession, freed from the notion of 'mine' and tranquil," the Bhagavad Gita teaches, "one is thus fit to become one with the Supreme." Christianity teaches that there are seven capital sins: sloth, anger, lust, pride, greed, gluttony, and envy.

"The pursuit of knowledge for its own sake," Albert Einstein wrote, "and an almost fanatical love of justice and the desire for personal independence—these are the features of the Jewish tradition which make me thank my stars that I belong to it." What calls us to our deepest, most impassioned selves is surely the really sanctifying dimension of religion for us. That which magnetizes us is the point at which our own holiness lies.

❧

Ralph Waldo Emerson said, "God enters by a private door into every individual." The problem with religious oppression or conversion by the sword is that one tradition assumes that it knows the door that is right for everyone else. But God's ways are not our ways, and God has a way for each of us that is different from the ways of those others around us.

❧

"We shall show then our signs on the horizons and within themselves," the Koran teaches, "until it becomes clear to them that it is the Truth." And the Judeo-Christian tradition teaches in Psalm 19, "The heavens are telling the glory of God and the firmament proclaims God's handiwork." The Spirit has clearly shown us the greatness of this God who speaks to us in everything.

❧

"Hear O Israel: the Lord our God is One," we learn in Deuteronomy. And the Hindu prays, "He is the one God, hidden in all beings, all-pervading, the Self within all beings." And the Sikh says in the Mul Mantra, "He is the Sole Supreme Being, of eternal manifestation." Clearly, the whole world knows that our God is their God, too. So how can we be more loved than they?

❧

"The Infinite is the source of joy. . . . Ask to know the Infinite," the Hindu Upanishads teach. The Talmud says, "The Holy Spirit rests on those only who have a joyous heart." And the Christian learns in Romans, "The Kingdom of God is not food and drink but righteousness and peace and joy in the Holy Spirit."

❦

The Koran says, "I have created the jinn [the angels] and humankind only that they might serve Me." And Paul teaches in Corinthians, "There is one God from whom are all things and for whom we exist." We are all under God, and we all know it. To harm the "other," then, means to harm someone whom God loves just as much as God loves us. So how is it possible to make war against "pagans" if there is no such thing?

❦

"Every being has the Buddha nature [the capacity for enlightenment]. It is the self," Buddhism teaches. The Judeo-Christian tradition says, "And the Lord said to Moses, 'Say to all the congregation of the people of Israel, "You shall be holy; for I the Lord your God am holy."'" African traditional religion prays, "O mighty Force, . . . Come down between us, fill us, Until we become like thee." We are made of stuff made to be holy because it is made from holiness. No religious tradition teaches a spiritual life of license or sin.

❦

"I have breathed into humans My spirit," the Koran says. "Let us always consider ourselves as if the Holy One dwells within," the Talmud teaches. "It is no longer I who live, but Christ who lives in me," Christianity says. But if we are all vessels of the divine, how can we use religion to justify destruction of other human beings?

❦

"Verily in the remembrance of God do hearts find rest," the Koran teaches. And we say, "Come to me all you who labor and are burdened and your heart shall find rest." God is the refuge of humans, the balm of all souls, the center of all life. Theirs as well as mine. And that's what is so hard to believe, isn't it, or else how could we be so sure that God is on our side alone?

59

❧

If we know all these things about our common understandings of creation, of life, of being loved by God, if we truly believe what is true in every religion, then we cannot fight religious wars, reject neighbors of another religion, make God our tribal God. "The best religion is the most tolerant," Delphine de Girardin wrote. Clearly, however we image God, one thing is certain: In God is all life. But if that is true, then to be intolerant in the name of religion is simply irreligious.

❧

Religious intolerance is one thing; religious respect for God's ways with other cultures, other peoples, the rest of creation is another. "My theology, briefly," Christopher Morley said, "is that the universe was dictated but not signed." God is many faces to many people—but all the same God.

❧

"I have just three things to teach: simplicity, patience, and compassion," the Tao Te Ching teaches. "There are only three things that matter: faith, hope, and love. And the greatest of these is love." Wouldn't the world be different if we all loved what God loves—the other?

❧

Denominationalism—the idea that we and we alone are saved, loved, blessed, talked to by God—has destroyed the word of God, fostered racism, and stained the world with religious blood. It makes God a commodity of our own design. Montaigne put it this way: "Oh senseless man, who cannot possibly make a worm, and yet will make Gods by dozens."

"When you are laboring for others, let it be with the same zeal as if it were for yourself," Confucius taught. Oh, no! I thought the real message was "Do unto others what you would have others do unto you." But then I found out that the Jews took that one, too. Now I don't know how to stay Catholic in the face of the competition.

A crowd of Catholics showed up at the gates of heaven. "Right this way," said St. Peter and showed them to a room. Later that day, Buddhists came, Presbyterians came, the Sikhs arrived, and then the Muslims. "OK," Peter said, "Now everybody's checked in, and we can get you all settled. But please tiptoe past the third room on the right." "But why?" the crowd said. "Because that's where the Catholics are," Peter said, "and we don't want to disappoint them; they think they're the only ones here."

When Is
Care for the Self/
Care for the Other
Excessive?

Matthew 22:39

You shall love your neighbor as yourself.

I found myself in conversation recently with what turned out to be a young immigrant family. The nation from which they spring has suffered a great deal throughout history. For years, the country was suppressed, subjected to colonialization, placed under military rule.

The people themselves knew abject poverty, public ridicule, and starvation. Many of them emigrated to other parts of the world. Though the worst of the foreign control and its oppressive restraints happened decades ago, this particular family had come here to escape the lingering effects of them—the lack of civic development, the loss of resources, the limited economic opportunities. And in the ten years they've been in the United States, they have done very well indeed. Well enough to vacation in exotic resorts, for instance. Well enough to own their own home in an affluent part of the city. Well enough to send the young mother and children back home to visit for several months every year.

The young man owns his own business now in a large American city where, he acknowledges, his ethnic connections made it possible for him to circumvent the usual training routines and apprenticeships. He "knew" people. He was the "right" color and kind for the situation. He "made" it. With just a little help when he needed it most, he made it.

The interesting thing is that he does not now approve of legislation that provides special support systems for minorities or mandates minority hiring practices. He thinks, apparently, that everyone should talk and work and look and think like he does. And most of all, everyone should make it the "hard" way, the way he did, he argues, forgetting that he himself had had quite a bit of support, in fact.

Listening to him, I remembered a story from the Hebrew Scriptures that, I realized, had never made much sense to me until I found myself with a person I was sure would understand the needs of the underprivileged people around him. But didn't.

In the story of the Tower of Babel, the writer tells of a nation—"of one language and one word set," the Scripture defines them—who set out to get ahead of everyone else by building a very high tower, "its top in the heavens."

When Yahweh saw what the people were doing, he knew that this would only be the beginning of their self-sufficiency, their parochialism, their control, their arrogance. So he "baffled" their language. He broke them up into small groups, in other words, so that each group would develop independently of the others, different from the others. He made sure that no one people would be the norm of human progress and development.

That way no single idea would reign, no single power would control the world, no single culture would mold the human spirit, no single set of ideas would limit the human mind. Then, everyone would have to learn from everyone else. Then everyone would have to reach out, reach down, reach across the limitations of language to connect with the other, to support one another. Then, simply to live, we would have to "love the other as ourselves."

❧

There is no such thing as care for the self that does not include care for the other. When we sweep the front stairs and the sidewalk in front of our own house, it raises the level of the neighborhood for everyone else as well.

❧

There is no such thing as care for the other that does not include care for the self. When we lobby for child care centers for the children of working parents, we assure ourselves an educated population for the future of our own town.

❧

There is no such thing as the unconnected self; there is only the selfish. We do not live in a vacuum, independent of the rest of the world. We only like to think we do. Rabbi Hillel wrote, "If I am not concerned for myself, who will be for me? But if I am only for myself, what good am I?"

❧

There is a difference between caring for the self and being uncaring of others. The two are not synonyms. The two are not compatible. What we do to others, does redound to our own benefit—and to our loss as well.

❧

People treat us the way we treat them. Snarl at the clerk and see who gets waited on first the next time. Smile at the clerk and see who gets waited on first the time after that.

❧

What we do for another individual we do for the society at large. There is no such thing as being able to do nothing to change the world. As Marie Curie put it, "You cannot hope to build a better world without improving the individuals."

❧

Self-sacrifice is meant to be a discipline that requires us to become our best selves. It is not meant to be an exercise in masochism. We sacrifice ourselves for those things that bring out the best in us, not the least, not the ignoble, not the undignified.

❧

To "sacrifice" the self is only holy when I become more for doing it. More of a fully developed human being, more of a committed professional, more of the kind of husband I want to be, more of a loving wife. To "sacrifice" the self at the expense of those things is to live half-fulfilled and resentful. There is no care for the other in that.

❧

"First, become a blessing to yourself," Raphael Hirsch wrote, "so that you may be a blessing to others." Please, spare us—no sad saints. If you don't want to do it, don't do it whining, sulking, and muttering as you go. Just explain kindly why this doesn't work for you and get on with life— for all our sakes.

❧

How do I know when I'm doing enough? That's easy. When there is nothing else I can do. Dag Hammarskjöld wrote, "You have not done enough, you have never done enough, so long as it is still possible that you have something to contribute."

❧

The rabbis teach, "If you want to know if your work on earth is finished and you are still alive, it isn't." You're not ex-cused from being human just because you're young or just because you're old. Every age has something to give. Demand it of yourself.

❧

When we cater to another, when we fawn, we do a disservice to the other. When we cater to the self, when we overindulge in anything, we do a disservice to ourselves.

❧

To be a fully developed self is to remain comfortable in our own choices and opinions while never undermining or ridiculing the choices and opinions of another.

❧

To care for another is to learn something ourselves—about life, about ourselves, about our talents. "Anything done for another," Pope Boniface VII wrote, "is done for oneself." If we remembered this, we wouldn't do so much complaining when we did it.

❧

It's important to be able to say no, yes. But what is more important is to know why we said no. It's not what we do that marks our character but why we do it that really says something about who and what we are.

❧

The important thing in life is to be able to strike a proper balance between caring for the self and caring for the other. But balance is not simply about arithmetic—about the number of hours we spend or the service we give. Balance is about doing a proper amount, a necessary amount, of both.

❧

We don't help other people by running ourselves into the ground, true. But we don't do anything for our own development by refusing to do what is necessary for another in order to do what is nice for ourselves.

69

❧

The self is a prison of infinite smallness, of minuscule confinement, of suffocating narrowness. It is only by learning to see beyond itself that the self becomes fully alive.

❧

Neither getting nor giving alone defines the meaning of life. But when we find ourselves on either end of that spectrum, something is surely wrong.

❧

To be forever intent on doing for another simply in order to receive the praise or approval or acceptance of others is to lack an inner self. No amount of self-giving can possibly replace what we lack in self-development. Anaïs Nin wrote, "She lives on the reflections of herself in the eyes of the other." How sad.

❧

The self that is satisfied is at peace with the world. Lao-Tzu counseled, "Manifest plainness, embrace simplicity, reduce selfishness, have few desires." Then it is not possible to be consumed by emptiness.

❧

When we spend more time on others than others either need or want from us, maybe we have to ask ourselves what it is in us that is lacking. The psychiatrist Thomas Szasz wrote, "The proverb warns that, 'You should not bite the hand that feeds you.' But maybe you should, if it prevents you from feeding yourself."

❧

Yes, Jesus poured himself out for others. But he also went to parties, had breakfasts on the beach, went into the desert by himself, and took time off from the crowds. What kind of spirituality is it that makes us feel guilty for doing the same? "The divine religion," Yehudah Halevi wrote, "does not urge us to lead an ascetic life, but guides us in the middle path, equidistant from the extremes of too much and too little."

If you want to know if you really "love the other as yourself," ask yourself if you have done everything you can to make sure that everyone else in society has what you have—and take for granted: insurance, food, housing, a job, education.

If you want to know if you love yourself enough, ask yourself how much time you take to do what you like to do.

If you want to know if you are, in fact, loving yourself at all, ask yourself if you have ever cultivated something you like to do—like crocheting or gardening or painting or golfing or music. Ever. And if you haven't, why haven't you? Listen carefully for the answer. It is the key to being a whole person; it is the key to a whole other life.

We can't do everything that needs to be done in this world, but we can each do something—like Meals on Wheels, or Red Cross volunteerism, or advocacy work on behalf of the poor, or environmental education programs. "Tsk, tsk" is not an answer to anything, and "Love your neighbor as yourself" was never intended to be an empty slogan. It requires that we begin to do something today.

If we aren't doing something to resolve the problems that plague society, as well as to attend to the damage they leave in their wake, it's very hard to argue that we really "love the other as ourselves." How long would you live in a house that leaked and do nothing but mop up the water every day?

Whatever we do on behalf of our own growth should make us even more valuable, more loving, more forgiving, more supportive of other people. "I change myself, I change the world," Gloria Anzaldua wrote.

"Life is ours to be spent, not to be saved," D. H. Lawrence wrote. That's an insight worth considering as we "save" our energy, our time, our selves, for the tomorrow, the position, the possibility that never comes. Better, perhaps, to give everything we have to make life here and now as good as it can be. For others as well as for ourselves.

It's always possible to do too much for people if we want them to become independent persons themselves. Or, to put it another way: One Sunday a cowboy went to church, but he and the pastor were the only ones present. The pastor asked the cowboy if he wanted him to preach as well as to pray. The cowboy said, "Well, pastor, I'm not the sharpest knife in the drawer, but if I went to feed my cattle and only one showed up, I'd feed him." So the pastor began his sermon. He talked for thirty minutes, sixty minutes, a full hour and a half. Finally, he finished preaching and came down to ask the cowboy how he liked the sermon. The cowboy answered slowly, "Well, pastor, like I said, I'm not the sharpest knife around, but if I went to feed my cattle and only one showed up, one thing I know for certain: I sure wouldn't feed him all the hay I had in the barn!"

How Does One Balance Patient Waiting and Action on Behalf of Justice?

Luke 18:11

And will not God grant justice to the chosen ones who cry out day and night?

Life is not lived in a straight line: Good is not always rewarded; evil is not always punished; justice is not always done. And goodwill is not always a substitute for virtue.

Innocent people die daily in death chambers around the world—including in the United States—while we try to save lives and deter murders.

The children of the poor go to school in deteriorating facilities and are treated to curriculums devoid of arts, music, and drama while we wonder why our inner cities have gone to spiritual sand.

Countries consistently use force to achieve justice and do more injustice in the process.

Children live without medical insurance in the richest country in the world while the federal debt deepens and lies beholden to militarism.

And, yet, interestingly enough, over the last century more people seem to have arisen intent on resolving problems like these than ever before in history:

Religious orders gave the Western world medical care, education, child care, and social service.

In our own time, the Green Party has become a political party aimed at helping the world live in harmony with nature.

Mother Teresa alerted the world to the destitution into which the world has sunk while, at the same time, it gets more and more technologically astute by the day and stock prices soar.

The peace movement tries to alert the world to the fact that war is obsolete, that there is nothing "just" about the unleashing of "strategic" nuclear weapons, that barbarism will never be over until the irrational becomes rational.

Yet, the violence goes on, the poverty increases, the oppression continues, and good people who would otherwise abhor such realities profit from them even while they deplore them. Nothing changes much. Except that violence gets more subtle, more efficient, and more invisible. For those who see, what is the answer to the implacability of it all? Should we stop trying and face reality? Should we give up and join the parade of profiteers and assume that if the human race gets rich one at a time, pretty soon everyone will be better off? Or should we accept the fact that life is evil and that there is nothing to be done about it but thank God that it's happening to someone else somewhere else? Should we simply be still and be glad it's not us?

The Sufi tell a story that has been my answer for years: Once upon a time, the story goes, a seeker ran through the streets crying, "Power, greed, and corruption! Power, greed, and corruption!" For a while people stopped to listen. Then, gradually, they all went back to the routines of the day. But the woman never stopped running, never stopped crying out, "Power, greed, and corruption! Power, greed, and corruption!" One day a small child stepped out in front of her. "Old woman," the child said, "no one is listening to you." "I know that," the old woman said. "Then if you know you're not changing anyone, why do you shout?" the child asked. "Oh, my child," she answered, "I do not shout in order to change them. I shout so that they cannot change me."

The answer is to stay the course, to bring the question, to demand an answer always to what it is in us that gives us tolerance for the intolerable, to give hope to the hopeless that someday, somehow, things will finally change.

Or, as Jesus put it, "I have prayed for you, Simon Peter, so that your faith may never fail and you in turn may strengthen others."

❧

To support the poor without devoting ourselves to eliminating the causes of their poverty is neither justice nor patience. Ministry without advocacy is no ministry at all. It simply perpetuates a sinful system.

❧

Justice is a condition of the heart as much as it is a social situation. When we stop taking injustice for granted, it will cease to exist. As it is, we assume that because sin is human, it must also be allowed to become an acceptable part of the civic or political arena.

❧

When the justice we seek does not come, it does not mean that we may cease the seeking. It simply means that there are not enough of us being persistent enough. The saying goes, "If you think your work is finished and you are still alive, it isn't."

❧

What we do not accept as either necessary or holy, what we refuse to be silent about no matter how understandable it may seem to everyone else—state violence, national famine, industrialized slavery, human degradation, sins against life— remains always a significant social question. Then we make both justice and patience of a piece. We strive for the right knowing that it is often long in coming.

❧

To give up and give in before justice comes is to have been poisoned by injustice ourselves. Then it really wins because it means that those who could see it have themselves gone blind.

❧

To seek justice is not simply to resist change or progress or necessary pain. It is to bring the great moral questions of the day to the bar of the soul.

❧

"Water wears away rock," the Chinese proverb teaches us. The truth is that many people seeking justice are seeking it differently than we ourselves do. We must trust that little by little, one person at a time, we can build a culture of peace.

❧

There are many ways of bringing the world to wholeness. Only by understanding that can we understand that people of goodwill often differ in their understanding of the best ways to achieve the same thing. "Those who are not against us are with us," Jesus tried to tell the apostles.

❧

To divide over which devices are most effective in the bringing of justice can simply be to practice another kind of violence. The philosopher Simone Weil wrote, "We should do only those righteous actions which we cannot stop ourselves from doing." It is endurance that is the key, not conformity of action.

❧

"Patient endurance / Attaineth to all things," wrote the great reformer St. Teresa of Avila. It is not success but unremitting witness that, in the end, makes the difference between revolution and reform.

❧

Burnout is a function of thinking that we must succeed rather than realizing that what we must really do is speak out and leave success to God. Or, as St. Catherine of Siena said, "Nothing great was ever done without much enduring."

When we allow injustice to go by unnoted, we create the climate for more injustice. Mother Jones, the great U.S. labor organizer from Cork, Ireland, put it this way: "Injustice boils in men's hearts as does steel in its caldron, ready to pour forth, white-hot, in the fullness of time." Eventually people have had enough. Then only those who give their anguish voice can save the fury that follows.

The difference between doing good for the oppressed and seeking justice for them is that those who seek justice seek to eliminate the causes of suffering as much as they seek to alleviate it.

Not to do justice, no matter how slow it is in coming, is to risk the entire human enterprise. Carrie Chapman Catt put it this way: "When a just cause reaches its flood tide . . . whatever stands in the way must fall before its overwhelming power." What age is there that has not known the truth of that?

We go on by going on. It is not a matter of scoring points. It is a matter of refusing to speak anything but the truth, no matter who says, "But at least things are better now than they have been."

Susan Griffin wrote, "There is always time to make right / what is wrong." To say "But it's always been this way" or "That is the way things are" is no excuse for injustice. If that were the case, then labor laws, slavery, illiteracy, and apartheid would be with us still.

❧

We are an instant-gratification generation. But we do not change heart as quickly as we change our ideas. The Italian proverb teaches, "Between saying and doing many a pair of shoes is worn out." That's why we keep on shouting whether people seem to be listening or not.

❧

Because life in a complex and changing society is confusing, the temptation is to stand still and wait for things to clear up, to wash out, to become right again. But that is not patience; that is indifference.

❧

"Thucydides," the student asked, "when will justice come to Athens?" And Thucydides answered, "Justice will not come to Athens until those who are not oppressed are as indignant about it as those who are." When we refuse to be patient, we are just; when we refuse to be intimidated by its delay, we are holy.

❧

As Bertrand Russell, the philosopher, put it, "The central problem of our age is how to act decisively in the absence of certainty." But injustice at any time is not an uncertainty and failing to act in the face of it is always wrong. It is possible to do nothing, but it is not possible to justify doing nothing.

❧

Archbishop Desmond Tutu taught us as we questioned whether it was any of our business whether there was apartheid in Africa or not, "When an elephant steps on the tail of a mouse and you say, 'I do not intend to take sides in this situation,' you have already taken the side of the elephant." Patience does not lie in ignoring the obvious; it lies in calling attention to it whether we can change it immediately or not.

❦

What we call patience in the face of evil is often convenience. As Marie-Jeanne Roland wrote, "It would have cost me more trouble to escape from injustice than it does to submit to it."

❦

To change the world, we must develop a spirituality for the long haul. We must learn to do what we can in our time, knowing that God's time may very well be different from ours.

❦

To say we want peace but continue to support wars that breed the anger that leads to the next one is to forget the lesson that led to the downfall of the Roman Empire: It is a great deal easier to conquer a country than it is to hold it.

❦

Patience is the ability to go on seeking the good even in the face of unremitting evil.

❦

To counsel patience in the face of human misery is to deny the will of God for all creation. It is one thing to endure evil while we work for good; it is another thing entirely to assume that the evil we face is all we can ever expect.

❦

Just because justice is a long time coming does not mean that we can simply sit back and wait for it to come of its own devising. Or, as the proverb says, "Time changes nothing; people do."

❦

On the one hand, as George Jackson wrote, "Patience has its limits. Take it too far, and it's cowardice."

On the other hand, as Augustus Caesar said, "Make haste slowly." Realize that it is not the statement of the ideal that changes the world; it is the ability to teach a new truth even while living with the dying of the old one.

Don't tell me what you hope for. Tell me what you are doing to bring it. Then you will know both patience and justice. As the poet Henry Wadsworth Longfellow wrote, "Let us then be up and doing, / With a heart for any fate; / Still achieving, still pursuing, / Learn to labor and to wait."

I heard a story once that gives me pause: The story goes that two old friends met on Main Street one morning, and one friend said to the other one, "Say, did you ever get that problem with the gas company solved?" And the second friend said, "Oh, yeah, it took a while, but it got settled." The first friend said, "I'm so glad to hear it. How did you do it?" His friend answered, "We compromised: They don't get any money, and I don't get any gas." Patience and justice may be of a piece, but both too often come slowly.

What Does It Mean to Be Faithful in the Face of Failure?

Psalm 78:1

Give ear, O my people, to my teaching; incline your ears to the words of my mouth.

Fidelity, perseverance, and persistence are not common civic values in a society that has come to take the instantaneous for granted. We compute life in nanoseconds now, not decades, not lifetimes, not eras. What cannot be done immediately either can't be done, we figure, or isn't worth doing. It's a "waste of time." And time is what we're all about.

We don't believe in seasons now. We force vegetables to grow in double time in hydroponic greenhouses. Or we freeze strawberries for serving in winter. We pile on academic credits, whatever the cost to either the breadth or the depth of the learning experience. The whole notion of sinking into something for a lifetime, until we exhaust it for ourselves or probe it to the core, is foreign to a culture in which change is the only really long-term expectation we have.

Most of all, we give up quickly on anything that takes months of cultivation or a lifetime of fidelity to bring to fullness. We are not people who specialize in intellectual bonsai trees, those little Japanese dwarfs of arrangements that bring a forest-full of beauty to a plot of land the size of a saucer, but only by virtue of the kind of patient pruning that is barely noticeable and always solemnly minute.

We bore easily. We quit quickly. We want immediate results. We succumb to the commonplace, to "Everybody's doing it," to "That's the way it is," to "What else is there to do?"

The long haul is, for most of us, a journey to be avoided at all cost. We want instant results, and we count our successes in terms of world-changing events, like winning the fight, or building the biggest, or changing the system, or converting the world. If we do not conquer what we set out to do immediately, we call it failure. But that is only because we fail to understand that what we undertake that does not yield may teach us more about us than anything else we do. When we understand that, we will have conquered the self.

The Baal Shem Tov spoke to his disciples about such persistence this way: "A man of piety complained to the besht, saying, 'I have labored hard and long in the service of the lord, yet I have received no improvement. I am still an ordinary and ignorant person.' And the besht answered, 'Ah, yes, but you have gained the realization that you are ordinary and ignorant, and this in itself is a worthy accomplishment, is it not?'"

Persistence and perseverance in hard times may not guarantee that we will achieve what we set out to do. But what we ourselves can become inside ourselves, in spirit and soul, in the process will be more than worth the effort.

❧

Fidelity to the cause itself, whatever its certainty or immediate accomplishment, may be what keeps the cause alive long after it seems to have failed.

❧

Those who persist in hard times are the only guarantee we have that what we hope for must surely someday be.

❧

Human growth is not an event; it is a process. "Failure," wrote Mary Pickford, "is not falling down; it is staying down." Just because what we set out to do does not yield to our efforts immediately does not mean that we have failed. It only means that both it and we need more attention.

❧

To be faithful to the process of failure is the first step in the process of success.

❧

Life is a journey of conversion. It is more important, in the end, that something happens in us to make us more authentic, more principled, more committed than that it happens to the systems around us, which must necessarily fade and pass, however perfectly we think we have shaped them.

❧

What each of us sets out to convert will in the end convert us as well.

❧

It is in being faithful to the deepest part of the self that we can become who we are really meant to be.

❧

The devils that rise to plague us in the process of commitment—impatience, boredom, frustration—are the mountains we must conquer in ourselves. "We are made to persist," Tobias Wolff wrote. "That's how we find out who we are."

❧

If our goals are too easily reached and our mountains too quickly conquered, it is possible that they weren't big enough aspirations to begin with. Life has to be about something big enough to work for without succeeding.

❧

Fidelity is what tells us that what we are doing is worth the risk of failing to achieve it. The Zen master teaches us to remember that "no seed ever sees the flower."

❧

Fidelity is not about being sure that what we commit ourselves to do will really get done. It is about not being sure at all but staying with the effort of it anyway so that the very model of commitment itself keeps the possibility alive.

❧

It's what we believe in, not simply what we do, that in the end becomes real, if not around us, at least in our own hearts.

❦

When the world lacks what the world sorely needs, it is only a matter of refusing to let the idea die that makes change possible. "Kill the snake of doubt in your soul," Kate Seredy wrote, "crush the worms of fear in your heart, and mountains will move out of your way."

❦

The sight of one believer makes the rest of the world pause and say, "Why not?" and "What if?" and "Of course." To see ongoing commitment in another makes us examine our own.

❦

Believers are not those who dabble in an idea to see if it's interesting. Believers are those whose soul is so aglow with the idea that they live it into life. We call them "obsessed," but, as a matter of fact, they're not obsessed; they're haunted by possibilities the rest of us cannot yet see—except through them.

❦

What is worth doing is seldom done easily. And sometimes, in fact, it must be done over and over again before it finally becomes commonplace. "You may have to fight a battle more than once," Margaret Thatcher wrote, " to win it." And who knows better?

❦

When we give up too quickly, too easily, too quietly, we may be responsible for letting the whisper of the Holy Spirit die not only in us but in our world as well.

❧

Sometimes it is better to relinquish a promise than to keep it without heart. Or, as Brigitte Bardot said, "It is better to be unfaithful than faithful without wanting to be." Fidelity is not meant to be an excursion into resentment.

❧

Where the heart does not reside whole, there is only duty, not fidelity.

❧

Fidelity is the fine art of remaining faithful to a vision that must come but is, for whatever reason, delayed.

❧

Fidelity hangs on when hanging on seems impossible, no matter how desirable. The prize fighter James Corbett put it this way: "You become a champion by fighting one more round. When things are tough, you fight one more round."

❧

To lose in the struggle to make the world better than what it is, is honorable. To quit trying just because winning does not seem possible is not.

❧

When we want something badly enough to refuse to admit that it cannot be, the whole world is given another chance to begin again.

❧

Realism and fidelity are not synonyms. Realism says it can't be done, and I must face that. Fidelity says it must be done, and I will do it.

❧

There are no such things as obstructions. There are only obstacles that slow the process and measure the quality of the fidelity. As William Ward said, "We can throw stones, complain about them, stumble on them, climb over them, or build with them."

❧

Dreaming does not make it so. Time does not guarantee anything. As Calvin Coolidge said, "Nothing in the world can take the place of persistence. Talent will not; nothing is more common than unsuccessful men with talent. Genius will not; unrewarded genius is almost a proverb. Education will not; the world is full of educated derelicts. Persistence and determination alone are omnipotent."

❧

The things we call impossible may only be one more step away from where we are right now. Don't stop trying too soon. "By perseverance," Charles Spurgeon said, "the snail reached the ark." That is not a comforting message to a people nurtured on the immediate, but it is very good nourishment for burning off fat from souls gone soft.

❧

It is not might that, in the end, shapes the world; it is persistence. As Edmund Burke reminds us, "By gnawing through a dike, even a rat may drown a nation."

❧

"A jug fills drop by drop," the Buddha taught. Only those who refuse to make the effort it takes to fill a dam drop by drop fail in the end.

Every day the man went to church and prayed to win the lottery. "God," he said, over and over again, "I've always been faithful to you: I went to church regularly, I prayed my rosary every day, I worked hard, and I tried to be kind to people. I need the money. But I never win!" He paused, waiting for an answer. Finally, he shouted into the shadows, "What else can I possibly do?" And this time a voice came out of the dark: "Buy a ticket, idiot!"

Before we can expect God to solve our problems, we must commit ourselves with the kind of untiring fidelity it takes to resolve them ourselves.

What Does It Mean to Be Enlightened?

Proverbs 1:20

Wisdom cries out in the street; in the squares she raises her voice.

L ife is about more than simply living and dying. It's surely about more than working for years. It's even about more, certainly, than being happy or unhappy, both of them qualities that stand to slip away with the shifting of the social wind. All of those things are real, of course. Each of them happens to all of us, sometime or other. Every one of them interrupts our lives. And everyone of them leaves us often adrift and disconnected from everything that went before it. Human development is a matter of shifts and changes, circles and turns. Certainty is rare in life; constancy is rarer still. So what is it that gives the kind of stability to life that enables us to weather each phase of life with serenity?

There are simply so many things in life that never get resolved. We grow old wondering if one of the children will ever really settle down. We grow up wondering if our parents will ever really get to like one another again. We live our lives wondering if we'll ever get back home, back to the state and the city and the neighborhood where we once lived and where we felt more secure than we've ever felt since.

Indeed, life is a series of permutations, all of them normal, all of them wrenching. But some people survive them and more. Some people move through life light of foot and smiling. Most people only prevail. In fact, few of us ever really collapse under the strain of it all. We take each moment as it comes, shrug our shoulders, and go on.

The question is, Why? How is it that some do it better than others? What is it, which, if carefully cultivated, can possibly bring ballast to all the moments of life? The answer lies in the awareness that there is more to life than survival. Life has a meaning beyond what we do, above what we become, in addition to what we are or even to what happens to us in the course of it. Serenity is the by-product of enlightenment.

Every major religious tradition speaks of some kind of enlightenment. To the Christian, it is union with God; to the Hindu, nirvana or freedom from all things; to the Buddhist, desirelessness; to the Muslim, submission to the will of God. In all of them, in other words, lies the consciousness that there is in us a tension between two opposing poles. At one level of life we seek only the gratification of the self for its own sake. At that stage we struggle against every period of life. At the other level, we achieve the transcendence of the self to the point where no external changes can disturb the balance of what we call the soul.

Enlightenment is not the characteristic of one kind of person only, the ancients teach. The Sufi tell the story of the disciple who asked the elder, "Holy One, why is it that the West got wealth and the East got wisdom?" And the Holy One said, "Because the West got to ask first." No one is more disposed than another to reach enlightenment, in other words. We can each achieve enlightenment, we can each come to wisdom, but only by virtue of the choices we make from moment to moment, from situation to situation.

We all start out at the lowest level of life, and we choose our way to enlightenment. Then, once we have become enlightened, whatever changes, whatever we lose in life, we lose nothing at all because things are not what control us.

St. Teresa of Avila put it this way: "Let nothing disturb you. Let nothing frighten you. All things are changing. God alone is changeless. Patience attains the good. One who has God lacks nothing. God alone fills all our needs."

❧

The awareness that we are meant to develop interiorly rather than simply exteriorly constitutes the beginning of enlightenment. Otherwise, we simply spend life chasing after things and positions and power and money. But none of them is either guaranteed or permanent. What could be more unenlightened than clinging to what is not permanent?

❧

In a society that ranks itself according to the amount of things a person can possess, we often confuse the wealthy with the wise. But it takes very little money to buy status. It takes a great deal of vision to gain enlightenment. "Wisdom," Goethe wrote, "is found only in truth."

❧

When we seek enlightenment, we seek the understanding that what we have managed to become in life outlives, outlasts, and outscores what we have managed to amass. Comfort seduces us into thinking that what we accumulate signals what we are. The Book of Ecclesiasticus teaches, "Wisdom is the wealth of the wise."

❧

It's not difficult to become smart. It is difficult to become enlightened enough to be able to distinguish what is smart from what is wise.

❧

What we have managed to achieve in life is no measure of enlightenment. Enlightenment has to do with what we manage to do without and still be happy. "Wise," the poet Edward Young wrote, "is to comprehend the whole."

⁂

When we come to understand that what we seek cannot be gained, it can only be valued, then we are enlightened.

⁂

"The way is not in the sky," the Dhammapada teaches, "the way is in the heart." Enlightenment starts here.

⁂

The Sufi say, "We have only what we cannot lose in a shipwreck." There is no truer definition of enlightenment. As long as our definition of ourselves has to do with what we have, we know nothing whatsoever about what it means to be completely human, completely free, completely enlightened.

⁂

To be enlightened, it is necessary to know how little enlightened we are. "The doorstep to the temple of wisdom," Charles Spurgeon wrote, "is a knowledge of our own ignorance."

⁂

The real social question of the age is, How many ads can a person possibly watch on TV and stay more committed to the enlightenment of the self than to the aggrandizement of the self?

⁂

This society tells us to feed our egos, our bodies, and our social situation. Enlightenment says that only when we let all of them go can we possibly ever be free of our addictions to them.

⁂

Confucius taught that there are three methods by which we can learn wisdom: through thought, through imitation, and through experience. It seems to me that one without the other two is vacant of credibility. Until we have gone through all of them, we are still dabblers at the gates of spiritual growth.

❧

Thought, Confucius implied, gives foundation to action. Unless I have thought through the values to be gained in any situation, I choose blindly. The one who is enlightened chooses consciously for altruism over profit, for depth of soul over the hoarding of things, for emptiness rather than a glut of superficial distractions that can only separate us from ourselves.

❧

Imitation, Confucius reminds us, reveals what we assess to be good. The people after whom we shape our own lives, the people who are our heroes, provide the clue to our own value system.

❧

Experience, Confucianism teaches, guides us through life at its dregs and provides the final test of enlightenment. Who we are on the other side of pain and loss is who we are at our best.

❧

I knew a young white man who, having been assaulted by two young black men, stayed forever frozen in prejudice and stereotypes. Given the opportunity to become enlightened about the nature of life, of humanity, of human weakness, he preferred the fantasy of his own superiority to the facts of the human condition. Cato the Elder wrote, "Wise men learn more from fools than fools from the wise."

❧

It's what we reach for, not what we have, that is the measure of our enlightenment. "Reach high," Ralph Vaull wrote, "for stars lie hidden in your soul." To seek enlightenment is to reach beyond our grasp.

❧

"God is always opening his/her hand," the Spanish proverb reminds us. To see God in every act of life is the beginning of enlightenment.

❧

There is no such thing as being enlightened about some things but venal about others. The Chinese proverb says it well: "The pine stays green in winter, wisdom in hardship." We can't play at being enlightened. Enlightened is what we are when life is difficult and we go on choosing only the best of attitudes at the worst of times.

❧

Enlightenment is the ability to forgo the fleeting satisfactions of the moment for the long, hard discipline of seeking always the best. "Destiny," Henri Frédéric Amiel wrote, "has two ways of crushing us—by refusing our wishes and by fulfilling them."

❧

Adversity sorts out what a person really is from what a person appears to be. The distance between the two is either spiritual enlightenment or superficial glitter. The Roman philosopher Seneca wrote, "We become wiser by adversity; prosperity destroys our appreciation of the right."

❧

Beware when you think you finally have it all. That is the invariable sign that you may not even have begun to get what is really important in life.

❧

Enlightenment does not lie in perfection; it lies in awareness. "To make no mistakes," Plutarch wrote, "is not in the power of the person. But from their errors and mistakes the wise and good learn wisdom for the future."

❧

We must remain always alert to those moments of insight that raise the soul above the material and open to us an understanding of what is really real—the qualities that last. "The soul," Emily Dickinson wrote, "should always stand ajar, ready to welcome the ecstatic experience."

❧

Enlightenment is a choice. We can choose to pursue the things that disappear with the passage of time, or we can choose to cultivate the qualities that transcend the vagaries of life. "The sublimity of wisdom," Jeremy Taylor wrote, "is to do those things living which are to be desired when dying."

❧

Enlightenment comes when we begin to sense the presence of God where once we recognized only the present in its most mundane of moments. Or, as Thaddeus Golas wrote, "Inside yourself or outside, you never have to change what you see, only the way you see it."

❧

Enlightenment comes when we begin to see all of life, and everything that touches us in it, in a new light.

❧

John Patrick wrote, "Pain makes us think. Thought makes us wise. Wisdom makes life endurable." On the other hand, enlightenment, the mystics show us, makes life meaningful.

❧

It's when we come to question our own insights that we may come closest to being enlightened. "It is unwise," Gandhi said, "to be too sure of one's own wisdom. It is healthy to be reminded that the strongest might weaken and the wisest might err."

❧

If you want to know if you are nearing enlightenment, simply ask yourself what you value in life, really value, can't even think of losing, would collapse if you no longer had it. What kind of thing is it? Is it something of the soul or something that's part of your social situation? "The art of being wise," William James wrote, "is the art of knowing what to overlook." What are you giving too much attention to now?

❧

Bernie stepped on one of those scales that tells you your fortune and weight and dropped in a coin. "Listen to this," Bernie said to his wife, showing her a small, white card. "It says I'm energetic, bright, resourceful, and a great lover." "Yeah," his wife nodded, "and it got your weight wrong, too." Enlightenment comes when we know ourselves as well as we think we know everyone around us.

How Can We Be Grateful in the Midst of Violence, Suffering, and Loss?

Psalm 107:1

Give thanks to God, for God's goodness and kindness endure forever.

Ome thing I've learned in life—the hard way and the long way unfortunately: There is a great deal of mystery in reality. My father died when I was three. Why such a thing would happen to a young mother and a small child is surely a mystery. My mother lived for twenty-eight years with Alzheimer's disease, and the mystery of it got deeper every day. I am at this moment sitting in an airport boarding lounge in Tokyo, the surety of today's flight long gone, an overnight delay a possibility, the length and difficulty of the trip a certainty. The mystery of such a hard ending to a long trip completely escapes me.

In fact, the real mystery is why such things happen at all. But the greater mystery may be what to think of them, how to handle them, how to deal with them spiritually. I found a story that provided some of the perspective it takes to embrace the mysteries of life, if not with "joy," at least with trust.

There were two monks, one somber and one joyful, each belonging to a different tradition, living miles apart. The first monk prayed all day long in deep, motionless silence. The second monk would sing and dance his praises to God near a huge tree in the monastery garden.

One day an angel appeared to the first monk and said, "I have come from God, and you have been given permission to ask God one question. What is your question?" The somber monk looked up and said, "How many more lives must I live before I will attain self-realization?"

The angel left him and reappeared miles away to the second monk who was singing and dancing before God. The angel said, "I have come from God, and you have been given permission to ask one question of God. What is your question?" Without hesitation, the joyful monk asked, "How many more lives must I live before I will attain self-realization?" And with that the angel disappeared.

105

One week later the angel returned to the first monk and said, "I have the answer you seek. You must live three more lives before you will attain self-realization." With that, the first monk fell dejectedly into heavy sobbing, "Three more lives, three more lives. Oh, no," he cried, "three more lives."

The angel left immediately and appeared to the second monk. "I have your answer. Do you see that tree around which you have been dancing and singing your praises to God?" "Yes," said the joyful monk. "You must live as many more lives as there are leaves on that tree before you will attain self-realization," the angel said.

The monk looked up at the tree and said, "Why, there must be ten thousand leaves on that tree. Only ten thousand lives? Only ten thousand more lives, and I will attain self-realization." And he began to sing and dance joyfully before God.

Suddenly a voice thundered from heaven, "My son, this day you have attained self-realization."

It's not always possible to rejoice in our struggles. But it is always possible to trust them. Then, we may surely give thanks, not for the blessings we have, but for the blessings we cannot see.

In every struggle, there is a hidden blessing. If my father had not died, I would never have discovered the Erie Benedictines. If my mother had not been ill for so many years, I would never have received the blessing of caring for her in her old age. If I hadn't been delayed in Tokyo today—well, the effects of that I don't know yet, but I have no doubt whatsoever that the blessing lurking there will somehow, someday become clear.

Think about your own struggles for a while and "give thanks to God."

❧

It is always easy to want things to be different than they are. It is always better to make the best of whatever is. To deal well with what we have is within our control. To change what is not within our control is impossible. To let it control us, then, is a tragic and serious mistake.

❧

Happiness is a choice, not an event. The attitude we bring to what we cannot change determines what will happen to us because of it.

❧

The creation of the unknown future belongs to God, not to us. Surely a good God is more to be trusted than our own limited plans and insights.

❧

The one best proof we have of the hidden gift in every great struggle is the fact that we survived the last one.

❧

Gratitude is not a reaction; it is a state of mind. When we go through life cultivating the ability to be grateful that it's not raining, that we are not sick, that we have good friends if not a lot of resources, and that we have found things we like to do, we are rich enough inside to sustain whatever we might lose around us.

❧

It isn't unreal to make the best of a bad situation. What is unreal is to demand that it be different.

❧

Better to be grateful for what is than to spend life in despair about what cannot possibly be. Despair simply means that we have given up on our own ability to make ourselves happy.

❧

Happiness does not come from outside of us. It comes from the ability to find enough within us to withstand whatever it is outside of us that threatens to destroy the equilibrium that makes life bearable.

❧

We learn gratitude only when we think there is nothing whatsoever to be grateful for. "No one," wrote Elie Wiesel, "is as capable of gratitude as one who has emerged from the kingdom of night."

❧

To be grateful and to be thankful are not the same thing. It's easy to be polite and not mean it. It's spiritual to be grateful, to do for another what has been done for us. "Thankfulness," Henri Amiel wrote, "may consist merely of words. Gratitude is shown in acts." To nourish a spirit of gratitude requires us to repay in kind what has been done for us.

❧

To know from the heart that what we cannot understand can nevertheless stretch us to heights beyond ourselves, frees us from needing to control all of life around us.

❧

One of life's greatest battles is the struggle for omniscience, for the cool, clear certainty of what is best for everyone at all times and the right to tell them so. Can you think of anything more miserable than insisting on the impossible at all times?

❧

If we can't have what we like, the only sane alternative is to learn to like what we have. Helen Keller put it this way: "So much has been given to me; I have no time to ponder over that which has been denied." And who is going to argue with Helen Keller—blind, deaf, and happy?

❧

Unhappiness comes from insisting that things be different from what they are. Sometimes justice demands that we demand a different world, of course. But until it comes, we must find within us the joy that comes from deep within and is impervious to external circumstances. "Those who are contented," T. C. Lai wrote, "are never poor."

❧

Those who thirst for justice want more for others. Those who are contented have enough for themselves and so have no need to take more than they need. The world owes both kinds of people a great display of gratitude. They save us from ourselves.

❧

"One ungrateful person," the Roman Syrus wrote, "does an injury to all who stand in need of aid." The point is clear: To treat the giver as if we were entitled to the gift makes gift-giving suspect. The more grateful we are for what we get, the more likely the giver will give to others as well. Gratitude, in other words, is itself a public service.

❧

We cannot expect the world to support us as if we are entitled to free service. We are entitled only to compassion—and even that requires that we pay its price in humility rather than the arrogance of entitlement and expectation.

❧

Gratitude does not demean us. It entitles us to the dignity that comes from graciousness. "No duty," St. Ambrose wrote, "is more urgent than that of returning thanks."

❧

"If you are really thankful," W. Clement Stone wrote, "what do you do? You share." That, I am convinced, is the difference between those who have and give and those who have but hoard. Thankfulness makes a person generous.

❧

To be grateful for what we have, even in the midst of want, turns poverty into another kind of riches. To be selfish in the midst of affluence turns wealth into a plague of greed. Then no amount is ever enough, and want eats out the center of the self.

❧

The mystery of gratitude lies in the fact that it has nothing to do with things. It has something to do with the quality of the human heart. William Ward wrote of it, "Gratitude can transform common days into thanksgiving, turn routine jobs into joy, and change ordinary opportunities into blessings." If you are miserable for what you do not have, ask yourself if what you are really lacking might not really lie within you.

❧

To be satisfied with what we have around us frees us to develop what is within us. All the museum tickets in the world will not make us art lovers if we have never cultivated the soul for it.

❧

To be grateful in the midst of want is to bless the God of the future rather than to worship at the feet of the present. It is the recollection that our good God who has sustained us in the past waits to give us new life, too, in days to come. The French say that "gratitude is the heart's memory."

We are given time only to learn the faith that enables us to relinquish it to a life beyond this one. God who has blessed us until now will bless us even more in days to come.

Don't be disturbed if you do not have everything you want. Just the ability to appreciate the good is often better than not desiring it. "I would rather be able to appreciate things I cannot have," Elbert Hubbard wrote, "than to have things I am not able to appreciate." It is possible, in other words, to become sated even on lobster. Better to have something only once a year, maybe, than every day if we are really to enjoy it at all.

Be careful what you want; beware of what you like. They say a great deal more about us than we too often realize. "The question is not what a person can scorn, or disparage, or find fault with," John Ruskin wrote, "but what we can love, and value, and appreciate." It is so easy to criticize what we have. Any fool can do it—and most fools do.

"For today and its blessings," Clarence Hodges wrote, "I owe the world an attitude of gratitude." There is no excuse for being sour about the bric-a-brac of life. If we are alive, that is more than enough.

"O, Lord that lends me life," William Shakespeare said, "lend me a heart replete with thankfulness." The operative word here, I think, is *lends*. What gives us the idea that we have a right to anything more than the time to come to grips with the real meaning of life? And the real meaning of life has nothing to do with the amassing of things, power, control, or status. It has something to do with coming to understand why we are here in the first place.

Beware the ingrates of life. They operate only on the basest of motives and the narrowest of ideas. "Gratitude," Aesop wrote, "is the sign of noble souls." These are the people who know that all of life is purely gratuitous.

"Let the man who would be grateful," Seneca wrote, "think of repaying a kindness, even while receiving it." If we are not intent on repaying a favor even as we receive it, it's time to wonder how it is that we began to believe that the world and everyone in it was put here for our service.

Do the Little Things Matter?

Ecclesiastes 1:2–3

Vanity of vanities, all is vanity.
What do people gain from all the toil at which they
toil under the sun?

There is a secret to the spiritual life. It takes long in learning—and too often comes late in life. But it is central. And it is key.

Every spiritual master in every tradition talks about the significance of small things in a complex world. Small actions in social life, small efforts in the spiritual life, small moments in the personal life. All of them become great in the long run, the mystics say, but all of them look like little or nothing in themselves.

The Zen master says, "The seed never sees the flower."

The Talmud tells the story of the well digger who said to the rabbi, "I am as great a man as you." And the rabbi said to him, "And how is that so?" And the well digger answered him, "When you tell the people to drink water that is ceremonially pure, it is I who provide it for them."

The Hindu says, "Just as a flower gives out its fragrance to whoever approaches it, so love within us radiates toward everybody and manifests in service."

The Sufi say, "Two reeds drink from one stream. One is hollow; the other is sugarcane."

Clearly, what we think are important things are always less than they seem and at the same time nothing is only what it seems.

To the Christian, Christmas itself, the birth of the Christ child, is the call to recognize the significance of smallness: to realize what each of us can and must become if we are ever to be fully human.

Our problem is that we are a culture of excesses: To the conventional wisdom, the largest cities are the best cities. The largest crowds are the sign of the truest position. The greatest amount of money is the indicator of the most happiness. The highest office is the mark of the most successful person.

But history tells us otherwise. We know that thousands followed Adolf Hitler in his scourge of Europe. We know that families have been rent to pieces in their struggles for the family fortune and that death, divorce, and disaster come to the wealthy as well as to the poor. We know that presidents and prime ministers, kings and corporate officers have been deposed and even destroyed just as easily, just as finally, as the underlings around them.

Life comes to us all in all its forms and everywhere.

What is most important is not what's "important" but what is "true."

Every morning an old lady came to the waterfront at low tide to throw back into the sea starfish that had been beached there by the receding waters of the night before. "Old lady," a young man shouted, "there are thousands of those things on this sand. What you are doing is useless." But the old lady said as she stooped down to save one more of the sea stars from certain death on the dry strand, "Not to the ones I throw back, it's not."

What matters, what's significant, is that we develop a vision that is greater than what the world around us thinks is significant.

Then, maybe we will come to understand the real miracle of Christmas: Jesus came to us as a child so that we might come to understand not only that nothing we do is insignificant but that every small thing we do has within it the power to change the world.

❧

To decide that simply because an action is small it is useless is to deny the effect of tiny drops of water on rock.

❧

Every single act of mine matters. Ask people who have lost elections simply because the people who were supposed to vote did not.

❧

Whatever small thing I do for another affects my own life also. The Hindus say, "Help thy brother's boat across, and lo! Thine own has reached the shore."

❧

Whenever we wait to do something that will make a difference, whether we realize it or not, we are making a difference by doing nothing at all.

❧

Doing what I can doubles the effect of everyone around me who is also doing everything they can. Marian Edelman, the child rights activist, wrote, "We must not, in trying to think about how we can make a big difference, ignore the small daily differences we can make which, over time, add up to big differences that we often cannot foresee."

❧

"If we stay on the road we are on," the Chinese proverb teaches, "we shall surely get where we are going." And in that lies both the victory and the defeat of everything. To persist in doing good, however small it seems, means that good will ultimately prevail. To do nothing for fear that nothing is possible because little is doable, is to assure the triumph of those who see no further than their own small desires.

117

❧

Listlessness and languor—the notion that either nothing can be done to make life better, or whatever must be done, I simply don't feel like doing it—do not belong at the Christmas crib. Christmas is about beginning the long, quiet journey to confirm the hope of the world—that it might become something greater than it is, one small step at a time. Leonardo da Vinci described the options: "I prefer death to lassitude," he said. In fact, lassitude is the death of the soul.

❧

What really matters in life is that something bigger than ourselves needs to matter to us. Then, though we may feel that we don't have much to bring to a problem, we will bring it all.

❧

We are not here to feed off the world. We are here to complete the world. And what is that? Well, Goethe said, "What, then, is your duty? What the day demands."

❧

None of us is given life for ourselves alone. We have all come to add what is missing in our world at the moment.

❧

There is no one who can solve it all, do it all, save it all. But together we can. All the comfort the world needs, all the generosity the people need, all the courage that is lacking in the world lie with us. "Service," the graffiti testified, "isn't a big thing. It's a million little things." The problem is that service fails when my piece of it isn't there.

❧

We have a choice: We can allow our littleness to be simply minginess of soul, or we can see it as a fountainhead of energy within us that calls us to realize that it is greatness of spirit we need to be successful, not an abundance of resources.

❧

The reason we see so few miracles in life is because we ourselves hesitate to make them happen because we are sure they can't. Or, as writer Henry Miller put it, "Moralities, ethics, laws, customs, beliefs, doctrines—these are of trifling import. All that matters is that the miraculous become the norm."

❧

Christmas calls us to remember that nothing important starts big. Everything—both good and evil—starts small. The problem may be that we never recognize either soon enough. After all, there weren't many people at the crib. Just the wise from both extremes in society.

❧

To determine what matters in life, just ask yourself what it is that, if allowed to continue, will have the greatest effect on the greatest number of people. And will it be for good or for ill?

❧

Significance and fame are not the same thing. Some of the most significant moments in our lives will never be recorded for public record. But we know what they are. As Anne Sexton wrote once, "It doesn't matter who my father was; it matters who I remember he was." Those are the things that we are required to pass on to those around us.

❧

It isn't deciding what must be done that's difficult. It's deciding that we must do it that's hard. We wait for someone else to take a thing in hand because we refuse to admit that the world is really waiting for us to do it.

❧

There is no great human question that does not take a local shape, live a local life. Where we are—people are hungry, violence is rampant, children have no health insurance, women get lower wages than men. The question is not, What can I do about it? The question is, Why am I not doing anything about it?

❧

It is hard to be smaller than Jesus of Nazareth. He was born in a manger. He was not a Roman tetrarch of Galilee. He was not the high priest of the temple. He was not wealthy, and he did not own lands. He was an itinerant preacher who saw the sick and served them, saw women and discussed great theological matters with them, saw institutional evil and refused to cooperate with it. So how do you and I stand at a manger and pray to be saved when we ourselves do little to bring salvation to others?

❧

Every word, every action, every effort of our lives has a ripple effect. Because of us, others will either do more or do less to co-create this world. "Every action of our lives," Edwin Hubble Chapin wrote, "touches on some chord that will vibrate in eternity." What do you want to hear played there on your account?

❧

There is no gesture so small that it does not have meaning to someone. As the poet Homer wrote, "The charity that is a trifle to us can be precious to others."

❧

It is rather simple in a technological society to seek fame. What is not easy is to become famous for doing something worthwhile for the rest of humankind.

❧

To live well in a world where people live poorly is no sin. The sin is not that so many are so rich. The sin is that so many are so poor. Then, we must each ask ourselves what we are doing about it. "Do you want to know if your work on earth is over?" the Sufi say. "Well, if you are still alive, it isn't."

❧

The crib asks the same question of everyone who approaches it: "Have you done for others yet what you are on earth to do?" That's a Christmas question that, without an answer, we have no right to celebrate.

❧

In the face of the manger in Bethlehem, who of us can say we have done all that we can do? "You have not done enough," Dag Hammarskjöld wrote, "so long as it is still possible that you have something to contribute."

❧

The poet José Ortega y Gasset wrote, "For the person for whom small things do not exist, the great is not great." Until we do what we ourselves are capable of doing for the world, we can never appreciate those who do even more.

❧

To be everything we can be, to do everything we can to make the world more just and more peaceful, is not simply a matter of doing something for others. The truth is that everything we do for others changes us at the same time we are changing them.

To give ourselves to the creation of the kind of world Jesus of Nazareth created around himself while he lived makes us more honest, more courageous, more sensitive, more wholly human as we go. David Jordan put it this way: "Be life long or short, its completeness depends on what it was lived for."

The significance of being part of something important in life—saving the whales, reforesting the mountains, empowering the powerless, confronting the powerful—lies as much in what we become as part of the process as in what we are able to do. "Life is not in having and getting," Matthew Arnold wrote, "but in being and becoming."

If we have become no different a person—no better a person—now than we were ten years ago, if life seems humdrum and rudderless, we have to ask what we have been about in life. "To give life meaning," Durant wrote, "we must have a purpose greater than the self."

It's so easy to blame God for the ills of the world, when it's what we do or don't do that is the real cause. Once upon a time, the Holy One sent his disciples to have a shirt made for a holy festival. "God be praised," the tailor said. "I will do a shirt for this wonderful event by a week from now." When the disciples went to pick the shirt up on the appointed day, the tailor apologized but the shirt was not finished. "God willing, I will certainly have it for you next week," the tailor said. But the shirt was not ready then, either. "If Allah blesses us," the tailor said to them, "I will surely have it finished next week." When the disciples told the Holy One about the delay, the teacher said, "Go back to the tailor and ask him how long it will take to make the shirt if he leaves God out of it." Waiting for God to solve what we are meant to do ourselves makes life one long unimportant enterprise. No wonder we get tired of living.